A Reader's Guide
to Haydn's Early
String Quartets

A Reader's Guide to Haydn's Early String Quartets

William Drabkin

Reader's Guides to Musical Genres, Number 1
Jeffrey Kresky, *Series Editor*

Greenwood Press
Westport, Connecticut • London

Library of Congress Cataloging-in-Publication Data

Drabkin, William.
  A reader's guide to Haydn's early string quartets / by William
Drabkin.
    p.   cm.—(Reader's guides to musical genres, ISSN 1523–0783
; no. 1)
  Includes bibliographical references and index.
  ISBN 0–313–30173–5 (alk. paper)
  1. Haydn, Joseph, 1732–1809. Quartets, strings.   I. Title.
II. Series.
MT145.H2D7   2000
785′.7194′092—dc21   99–11131

British Library Cataloguing in Publication Data is available.

Library of Congress Catalog Card Number: 99–11131
ISBN: 0–313–30173–5
ISSN: 1523–0783

First published in 2000

Greenwood Press, 88 Post Road West, Westport, CT 06881
An imprint of Greenwood Publishing Group, Inc.
www.greenwood.com

Printed in the United States of America

The paper used in this book complies with the
Permanent Paper Standard issued by the National
Information Standards Organization (Z39.48–1984).

10 9 8 7 6 5 4 3 2 1

Contents

Preface   vii

1. Introduction   1

2. Anatomy of the Quartet   9

3. Fugue   51

4. Quartet in F Minor, Op. 20, No. 5   69

5. Quartet in A Major, Op. 20, No. 6   81

6. Quartet in C Major, Op. 20, No. 2   91

7. Quartet in G Minor, Op. 20, No. 3   105

8. Quartet in D Major, Op. 20, No. 4   125

9. Quartet in E♭ Major, Op. 20, No. 1   143

10. Epilogue   161

Notes   167

Bibliography   179

Index   183

Preface

This book began as a study of Haydn's Op. 20 string quartets. No recent study of the Haydn quartets has focused on these works, and the appearance a few years ago of a handbook on Op. 50 provided the impetus to consider an earlier set of Haydn quartets in a similar forum. Soon after embarking on this project, however, I realized that by looking at these quartets in isolation I would be unable to convey my thoughts about them adequately. It was not simply that all great works must be studied in context, but rather that Haydn's prodigious achievements in Op. 20 are better understood in terms of his development as a composer of string quartets from the late 1750s, and particularly as the culmination of an intensive period of quartet composition between 1769 and 1772. It seemed odd to cut off a group of six quartets, written at a relatively early stage in the genre's history, from twelve others that are nearly contemporary with them.

I began this study from the premise that the appreciation of any Haydn string quartet, *as a quartet*, ought to be based on a consideration of the genre from a "theoretical" point of view, that is, considering the resources available to a composer writing music for two violins, viola, and cello and the historical precedents implied by the medium. Since Op. 20 was composed rather early in the history of the string quartet—few can have predated it by more than twenty years—it was necessary to look at a wider repertory to provide a base for a critical discussion of the set. This discussion is focused on the quartets Haydn wrote before 1772, but includes a few examples of later works by Haydn and Mozart. A detailed examination of every Haydn quartet before Op. 20 would have far exceeded the scope of my work, but using these works as the basis of a chapter on string quartet texture and technique—what I call an "anatomy of the quartet"—seems the most sensible way of defining those qualities that give the quartet its generic identity and appeal. They are, for me, the real background to Op. 20.

Some years ago, a seminal investigation of the early history of the quartet, by Ludwig Finscher, ended with a substantial study of "The Theory of the String Quartet." Finscher's achievement is prodigious, and remains indispensable for any serious consideration of the genre. It struck me as odd, initially, that a substantial section on "theory" should appear as the final chapter of a book tracing the progress of the string quartet to the year 1781 rather than as part of an exposition of analytical concepts and tools. It turned out, however, that Finscher's theory was essentially a study of the aesthetics of the quartet, its ethical values, and its effect on the attitudes of succeeding generations of composers, critics, and teachers. It included much discussion of "conversation" between players and musical "personalities" in the abstract, but did not actually relate any of this to specific contexts; this was symptomatic of a study that, with few exceptions, was more concerned with the external features of quartets—movement types, formal planning, general activity analysis—than with following the course of compositional ideas in individual works.

This study will attempt to steer clear of the debates over the point at which "great Haydn" (or, if you prefer, "good Haydn") begins and how his oeuvre is best divided into creative periods. Though I have never favored a historical equalization of composers or their works, the project has reaffirmed my long-held affection for Haydn's instrumental music from the late 1760s and early 1770s, and my belief that economy of means is a virtue in art.

The title of my study requires a brief explanation. For Haydn specialists, the "early quartets" are, simply, the ten quartets—sometimes called "quartet-divertimenti"—that the composer produced in the late 1750s and early 1760s, initially in response to an invitation from Baron Carl Joseph von Fürnberg to write something for "four friends of the art [of music]." These works, which are today identified under the rubrics "Op. 1" and "Op. 2," form a distinct group: each comprises five movements, with two internal minuets framing a central slow movement or, if the first movement is itself slow, a scherzo in 2/4. For most concertgoers, however, the two sets of six quartets that follow, known as Op. 9 and Op. 17, are unlikely to be better known than the ten of Op. 1 and Op. 2, though they were written about a decade later and, like all of Haydn's subsequent quartets, comprise four movements each: for this audience, Haydn's "early" quartets might be renamed the "unfamiliar" ones. If I may be allowed to use "early" in both senses at the same time, then it makes sense to include Op. 20 in the group, since it is the product of the same creative burst of energy that produced Op. 9 and Op. 17. At any rate, the subtitle of my book removes any ambiguity about its scope.

The broad plan is to lead from a discussion of string quartet texture and technique, exemplified mainly by Opp. 1, 2, 9, and 17, to a more detailed look at each of the six quartets of Op. 20. Inevitably, the study of whole pieces progresses beyond the identification and cataloguing of textures to observations on how changes of texture help shape pieces. In each of the chapters on the individual quartets of Op. 20, I start with remarks on musical form, to provide an orientation for more detailed discussion of texture and other techniques. In the final chapter, I consider ways in which the four movements of a quartet are bound together and explore how the opus as a whole may be thought of as an artistic unit. Bridging these parts of the book is a chapter on fugue, a major stylistic factor in the Op. 20 set that has no precedent in Haydn's earlier quartets.

Much of what I have written is, admittedly, concerned with details. Offering a series of close readings of musical passages is not normally a sure way of endearing the reader to one's thoughts, but in Haydn's case I can see no alternative: it is Haydn's attention to detail—his appeal to quartet players as musical connoisseurs—that elevates this music so far above the conventional. It is not my intention, though, to exhaust the reader by a comprehensive, bar-for-bar analysis of every quartet. For each movement of Op. 20 I have allocated space for only the limited number of features that I believe most worthy of close examination. None of the later chapters is very long, and each can be read independently of the others. I have also tried to be generous with musical exemplification, and to link my longer verbal arguments to the musical text with a system of lettered cues ((a), (b), (c), etc.). Finally, I have avoided putting forward arguments that I regard as "obscure"; nothing has been written here which I have not myself verified while listening to or playing these works.

Although I have written this book in such a way that it can "stand alone," that is, it contains sufficient musical exemplification to spare the reader flipping between text and score, my interpretations will be effective only insofar as they enhance the reader's appreciation of these quartets as a whole. For this, scores and performances (or recordings) of Haydn's quartets are indispensable. Excellent editions of Haydn's first twenty-eight quartets have been issued by the Joseph Haydn Institute in Cologne, under the directorship of Georg Feder, as part of the new collected edition of his works; these may, however, be beyond the means of the average reader. The traditional Eulenburg scores, reincarnated under the Dover Books imprint, are altogether more affordable and accessible, but are riddled with errors of all sorts—dynamics, articulation, rhythm and pitch, repeat signs, movement titles—and should be used with extreme caution. The most glaring of these errors are noted in my text; indeed, many insights into Haydn's quartet style came to me as a result of comparing the Haydn Institute's edition with the versions of the quartets with which I had grown up.

This book has not been designed to be read in one sitting. To do justice to works such as Op. 20 requires living with them for a while; if my arguments are persuasive or thought-provoking, then a perfectly adequate response to them would be to stop reading in order to reflect, to assess, to listen, to play. I am quite content, then, to offer my work as a handbook, a companion to Haydn's first twenty-eight string quartets.

I generally follow American spelling, usage and orthography; the few exceptions, e.g. "practise" (as a verb), "envisage" (rather than "envision"), "analyse," and "judgement," date from my years as a text editor for *The New Grove Dictionary of Music* during the 1970s. Italian performance markings have been italicized (e.g., *staccato, pizzicato, fortissimo*) but not elements of form or movement titles and tempos ("ritornello," "scherzo," "Poco adagio"). Haydn's spelling of "Minuet" changes to "Menuet" with Op. 9; I respect Haydn's spelling for the titles of movements but use "minuet" when referring to the type of movement generally.

Pitch-classes, i.e. notes that are not tied to a specific register, are given in upper-case type; thus, for example, "the key of D minor," "the open C string." The names of individual, i.e. *register-specific*, pitches follow the Helmholtz system, with middle C given as c^1 and octave registers reckoned from C to B. Thus, for example, the open strings of the cello have the pitches C, G, d, and a; those of the violin are g, d^1, a^1, and e^2.

A grant from the Humanities Research Board of the British Academy enabled the University of Southampton to extend a term's sabbatical to a full year's study leave in 1997. But the gratitude I owe the referees of my HRB application, Ian Bent and the late Derrick Puffett, extends beyond the letters of support they wrote on my behalf: their contributions to the literature of music theory and analysis have been a constant source of inspiration, and their encouragement of my work extends far beyond the bounds of this project. Thanks are also due to James Webster, whose influence on a generation of Haydn lovers has been inestimable and to whose repeated calls for a more sympathetic treatment of Haydn's early music this book is, I hope, received as a welcome response; to the Allegri Quartet, for their friendship and for enriching many generations of students in the appreciation of the quartet repertory; to Jeffrey Kresky, general editor of the series in which this book appears, for providing a forum for my work; and to Helen Greenwald of the New England Conservatory, for a critical reading of my typescript, which led to many refinements. Though I bear full responsibility for any shortcomings in my work, these scholars and musicians must share the credit for any help I offer here towards the understanding of Haydn's quartets.

I owe a special debt of gratitude—one that I scarcely know how to express in words, let alone repay—to my late father, I. E. Drabkin, the viola player in uncounted evenings of chamber music during my childhood, and a teacher of ceaseless devotion and patience.

1

Introduction

On the whole, Haydn's first twenty-two quartets—those up to and including Op. 17—have fared badly in the musical world. They are rarely played, and not often discussed in the literature except when surveyed in a study of his quartet output purporting to be comprehensive. The first ten of these, which have been assigned numbers in Op. 1 or Op. 2, have even been said not to be true quartets, but merely works that just happen to have been written for the combination of two violins, viola, and cello.[1]

Misunderstandings about the canon and chronology have contributed to the well-known historical viewpoint that Haydn's Op. 33 marks the first maturity of the Classical quartet. The works grouped under Op. 1 and Op. 2 have been dated as early as 1750 and as late as 1763; a further set of six early quartets, known as Op. 3, were assigned to the year 1767. Given a steady stream of works up to 1772, it was easier to relegate Op. 20 to the category "early Haydn" despite the fact that several Op. 20 quartets secured a foothold in the repertory. The nine-year gap between Op. 20 and Op. 33 thus gained a special significance in Haydn's development as an artist, giving him an opportunity to take stock of what had been achieved up to 1772 and to consider the stylistic refinements that were still required. That Haydn himself referred to Op. 33 as having been written in "an entirely new and special way," acknowledging in the same breath a long hiatus in quartet composition, lent further credence to its seminal position in his oeuvre.

We are now quite sure, though, that Op. 3 is not part of the Haydn canon, and modern scholarship has also put the date of Op. 1 and Op. 2 at around 1757–62; thus there are several gaps in the chronology of Haydn's quartets.[2] In Table 1.1, spaces indicate a break of several years between sets of quartets or some other change in the rate of productivity:

Table 1.1
A summary of Haydn's quartet output

Traditional numbering	Number of works	Composition date
Op. 1 and Op. 2	10 quartets	ca. 1757–62
Op. 9	6 quartets	ca. 1769–70
Op. 17	6 quartets	1771
Op. 20	6 quartets	1772
Op. 33	6 quartets	1781
Op. 42	1 quartet	ca. 1785
Op. 50	6 quartets	1787
Op. 54/Op. 55	6 quartets	1788
Op. 74	6 quartets	1790
Op. 71/Op. 74	6 quartets	1793
Op. 76	6 quartets	1797
Op. 77	2 quartets	1799
Op. 103	quartet fragment	1803

According to Table 1.1, Haydn enjoyed two especially intensive periods of quartet composition, 1769–72 and 1787–97, but there were long periods of silence not only before Op. 33 (nine years), but also before Op. 9 (at least seven years) and Op. 50 (six years, disregarding the single short quartet known as Op. 42). It is possible to lay a claim for each of these sets as marking a new artistic level in Haydn's art of quartet composition. Indeed, Robbins Landon, in introducing the quartets of 1769–72 to the readers of his five-volume *Haydn: Chronicle and Works*, unwittingly parodies the composer's famous remark about Op. 33 when he writes that "Op. 9 was constructed in an entirely new manner."[3] The table also shows Op. 33 as historically isolated, the only set of six quartets that is both preceded and followed by a long gap; that viewpoint is at odds with the claim voiced by many historians that this opus marks the defining moment in the Classical quartet.

The tendency of historians to dismiss the quartets before Op. 20 is matched by a general reticence to consider them worthy of extended discussion. Virtually every account of Opp. 1, 2, 9, and 17 forms part of a larger survey of Haydn quartets, and lumps them together as work-in-progress towards a later goal. Their neglect by analysts and theorists is even more striking. Hans Keller's monograph on the analysis and performance of Haydn's quartets is restricted to what the author calls the "great" quartets, and deliberately neglects all but one of the quartets before Op. 20 without explaining why they have no place in the book.[4] Few studies treat any of the first twenty-two quartets as serious works of art.[5]

What I am offering here may be called "analytical" insofar as it is concerned with showing how individual quartet movements are put together and how they create their effect on their own terms. It is nevertheless based upon a few historical observations. First, the string quartet developed, in a very short space of time, from a number of well-established sources—symphony, trio sonata, aria—to a genre of its own in the front rank of instrumental music. The first pieces of any sort for two violins, viola, and cello cannot have been written much before the mid-1750s, and the early quartet is often difficult to distinguish from, say, the string parts of a mid-eighteenth-century symphony. By the 1770s, however, Haydn's quartets were being imitated by promising composers, including Mozart, specifically as models of string quartet composition.

Second, as the quartet took shape it became a musical metaphor for conversation among educated persons, with its attendant notions of intimacy, the exchange of ideas, and of individual personalities for each of the four members in the ensemble. The tradition of perceiving the quartet as a conversation goes back to the 1770s, but the most famous pronouncement along these lines was made by Goethe late in his life: "The string quartet is the most comprehensible genre of instrumental music. One hears four intelligent people conversing with one another, believes one might learn something from their discourse and recognize the special characteristics of their instruments."[6] Goethe's suggestion that the conversation will impart to the attentive listener something of the characteristics of the instruments uncannily echoes a remark ascribed to Beethoven from only a few years before. According to Karl Holz, a violinist who was friendly with the composer and who played in some of the first performances of the late quartets,

When he [Beethoven] had finished the Quartet in B flat, I said I thought it was indeed the best of the set comprising Opp. 127, 130 and 132. He replied: "Each in its own way! Art does not permit us to stand still" (he often used the royal "we" jokingly). "You will notice a new type of part-writing" (by this he meant the distribution of tasks among the instruments) "and there is no less imagination than ever before, thank God."[7]

Both quotations are concerned with the quartet as "instruments": what they are capable of doing and how they respond to each other in a musical argument. And the quotes gain in force by having been written at a time in which quartet playing had ceased to be an exclusively private or semiprivate activity: Goethe compares listening to quartets with hearing a concert by a virtuoso artist; Beethoven addresses a musician who was involved in rehearsals and performances of some of the most difficult music hitherto written for string players. And yet they seem to take us back to an earlier age in which quartet playing imitated "conversation," when performers were sensitive to the ways in which these conversations took place.

If we take these two points together, we could say that the string quartet obtained its identity by creating musical conversations, through techniques of solo writing, in eighteenth-century compositional style. There is, of course, nothing radical about this view of the genre: the string quartet has always been talked about in terms of conversation and of the interdependence of four soloists. But there is as yet no theory that has been devised specifically for the string quartet, that is, a method of approaching quartets that is primarily concerned with what four string instruments are capable of doing and how they work best together.

Consider, for instance, the first minuet of Quartet in B♭, Op. 1, No.1 (Example 1.1). Though the work is hardly known to concertgoers, it enjoys a certain symbolic cachet as the progenitor of the Classical quartet by virtue of its opus number and the account of one of Haydn's early biographers.[8] At first sight, there does not appear to be much to say about this minuet. Its form is a straightforward a–b–a form; the last ten bars, not reproduced here, are an exact repeat of the first ten. The a-section remains in the tonic, while the b-section develops harmonically by moving to the dominant and thematically by rearranging the pairs of eighth notes in an ascending pattern. The texture is mainly three-part, with the course of the second violin largely determined by that of the first. Nor can it be called "conversational": the viola rarely breaks free of the bass line, and the texture is reduced to two parts at what ought to be the climax of the piece. In the apparent absence of independent motivic interest in the inner parts, how could this piece be said to embrace the genre of string quartet?

To answer this question, it is worth noting at the outset that the trio sonata is an important forerunner of the quartet and that we should therefore not be surprised to see long stretches of trio-sonata texture embedded in Haydn's early quartets. It is, then, more interesting to examine those passages in which Haydn departs from this model.

Look first at the viola part. In all, it differs from the cello for just two bars, at *(a)*. But these bars provide the fulcrum for the minuet: not only does the change from three-part to four-part harmony take place in the middle of the modulation to the dominant, but there is also something gently unsettling about a consequent phrase answering an antecedent with a palpably fuller texture, almost as if the effect of a sudden *forte* were intended at bar 13. In other words, we could view the piece passively as a trio in design, or we could applaud Haydn for his delay in realizing the full potential of the quartet by withholding full four-part texture until a point of greater harmonic tension is reached, and even for overshooting this point, subversively, by two bars.

The second violin part shows further subtle changes of texture. In the first four

Minuet

Example 1.1 Op. 1, No. 1, ii, bars 1–24

bars, it keeps within the general trio texture by following the first violin at the interval of a tenth; this interval is reduced to a sixth and later to a third, as the first violin part continues to descend. But although the contours of the two violins depend upon one another, the second divides its allegiance texturally between the first and the lower instruments. At *(b)* it cannot imitate the chromatic movement f–f♯–g above it, so it instead contributes to the repeated notes below. And when the first violin becomes more soloistic by including triplet figures in its part, the second aligns itself still more closely with the accompaniment, for example, by resting on the third beat of the bar at *(c)*. After the double bar, it recedes entirely into the accompaniment for four bars, but emerges surprisingly at *(d)*, as the bass line of a two-part texture. Within a short space of time, then, the second violin acts in turn as a secondary melodic line, as a nondescript inner part, and as a bass. Moreover, its changes of role correspond with different dynamic states in the music: the neutral presentation of the main theme, the shift away from the home key at bar 11, and the cadencing in the new key of the dominant in bars 15–18.

The ensuing six bars of retransition appear to be a negation of the chamber music ideal: not only are the viola and cello paired once again, the two violins also play in unison (or, according to some early sources, in octaves). This must not be seen as an impoverishment of the quartet, though, but rather as an enrichment: the two-part texture of bars 19–24 imitates contemporary orchestral sonority, and thus contrasts effectively with the chamber texture of the violin duet heard in the previous bars. It is the variety of textures used here—chamber versus orchestral, few parts versus many parts—that elevates this minuet above much other four-part music.

The changes in the second violin and viola parts that I have just discussed are fairly easy to describe, and may not even be the sort of thing that engages our attention. Most listeners perceive string quartets as coming from a single "source," whether a concert hall stage or a wall supporting two loudspeakers. When they hear a performance of this minuet, they are apt to experience the second violin in bars 15–18 as a shift of the bass line into a higher octave, from f to f^1. From within the quartet, however, the experience can be far more vivid: the second violin may interpret it as a break from the tedium of having to play below the first (literally "playing second fiddle"), while the cello may be annoyed to find its role in the ensemble usurped by a melody instrument, one that is inherently unsuited to playing bass parts! Our assessment of the early quartet is hampered by the separation of listener and player; indeed it is hard to imagine a professional quartet conveying the issues described here to an audience of many hundreds of people, most of them seated far from the concert hall stage.

Nothing I have proposed about Haydn's "first" quartet minuet is intended to imply that the early quartets deserve to be elevated to a central place in the concert repertory. What I am suggesting is that, as chamber music, this minuet exhibits a high degree of competence in its own right: it is an artistic creation of the 1750s by a composer of the first rank. Much of what we take for granted as part of Haydn's so-called mature quartet style can be traced back to these and other early works. It is the purpose of the next chapter to investigate the terms of reference of the mid-eighteenth-century quartet and to see how they function in context.

2

Anatomy of the Quartet

History continually reminds us how one generation of composers absorbs the works of past masters. In the realm of the Classical string quartet, the genealogy has been traced many times. In Mozart's early quartets one can see movements from Haydn's quartets of 1769–72 used as specific models; in his set of six quartets of 1782–85, which he dedicated to Haydn, Mozart made his debt to the older master perceptible on many levels. Beethoven, whose mission as a young man was famously described by his friend Count Waldstein as the acquisition of "Mozart's spirit from Haydn's hands," did not try his hand at string quartets until he was in his late twenties but made copies of quartets from Haydn's Op. 20 and Mozart's "Haydn" set. His first quartets, Op. 18 (1798–1800), appropriates techniques from Mozart but also shows many subtle connections with Haydn. In the early nineteenth century, composers also looked at Beethoven's quartets for examples of technique and texture. Mendelssohn, writing his first string quartets between the ages of eighteen and twenty, took inspiration from Beethoven's middle- and late-period quartets; the "borrowing" in Op. 13 in A minor (1827) of a recitative-like passage from Beethoven's own A minor quartet (Op. 132), composed only two years before, is perhaps the most famous example; the Adagio non lento of the same work contains more pointed references to the slow movements of Beethoven's Op. 95 and Op. 130, and Mozart's Quintet in G minor, K. 516. These examples testify to more than a tradition of quartet composition stretching back to the middle of the eighteenth century: they bear witness to a line of composers eager to assimilate the best practice of what had preceded them. But while connections between great scores affirm and renew our faith in the study of music history, they do not alone provide us with a basis upon which to comment specifically on what has been worthy of emulation, that is, to analyse the noble achievements of the past. For this purpose, we turn to music theory.

To many observers, there might already seem to be enough theory around for the purpose of undertaking this analysis. There are theories of harmony (tonality, chord progression) and counterpoint (consonance and dissonance treatment, relationships between parts, thematic process and form) as well as unified theories that show how the various parameters of music—tonal, thematic, formal—are harnessed together. To some extent the Classical quartet may be subjected to the same types of analytical inquiry as other music of the period, especially instrumental music. Its movement types are similar to those encountered in solo sonatas and symphonies, including sonata forms, variation sets, minuets, and scherzos with trios of a lighter character. It explores the possibilities of thematic development and the sharing of thematic interest among the parts; the quartet can, naturally, make the sharing of thematic material a more prominent feature of its musical surface, though its slow movements tend to favor a melodic line in the first violin as a dominant lyrical voice. Phrase structures and harmonic patterns are also similar to that found in other genres, and it uses contrasting materials as much as thematic development as a way of advancing a musical argument.

Yet quartets are different from keyboard instruments and from the orchestra, and composers have long recognized that the differences among these media are sufficient for the nature of composition to change. When Haydn made a keyboard arrangement of the finale of his G major quartet Op. 33, No. 5, a set of variations on a *siciliano*, he omitted the second and third variations, the very parts of the movement (about two-fifths of its length) in which thematic interest is shifted to the inner parts. He also found it necessary to ornament the theme and to modify the left hand in the concluding *presto* in order to avoid the rapid restriking of keys. The result is a movement of considerably less variety, and at the same time one whose origins as a string quartet would be difficult to imagine were the original not so familiar. In the reverse process, the Beethoven arranged one of his early piano sonatas—Op. 14, No. 1—for string quartet shortly after the appearance of Op. 18, yet within months of its publication in 1802 he came near to regretting what he had done, decrying "the unnatural mania, now current, for transplanting even *things for piano* into the medium of string instruments, instruments which in all respects are so utterly different from one another," and further stipulating that "not only would whole passages have to be entirely omitted or radically altered, but some extra material would also have to be included."[1]

The purpose of this chapter is to outline a theory of quartet texture, to help us explain how material is distributed among the four parts and how these parts interact with one another. It is intended, in short, to provide a basis for analysing quartets as quartets, and not just any piece that happens to be written "in the Classical style."

It would be worth starting on a cautionary note regarding Beethoven's remarks about the piano and string instruments being "utterly different from one another." The beginning of the first-movement development section of Haydn's Op. 9, No. 1 is given as Example 2.1. Taken out of context, and heard by ears more familiar with Haydn's better-known quartets, the unashamedly pianistic style of accompaniment—it continues in the same vein for another four bars—gives the impression of being arranged from a sonata for violin and keyboard, with the "right hand" broken chords of the accompaniment being shared by the inner parts of the quartet. Were this characteristic of Haydn's early quartets, it would be grounds for dismissing them as immature.

Example 2.1 Op. 9, No. 1, i, 31–32

This sort of texture is not found anywhere else in Haydn's first twenty-two quartets, yet it returns in later works: longer passages of broken chords in a keyboard idiom are found in the opening movement of Op. 20, No. 2; the slow movement of Op. 33, No. 5; and the variation movement of Op. 64, No. 4—works which have long been accepted as masterpieces of the genre. But it is a mistake to say that "pianistic" idioms are by definition out of place in the string quartet; they are among the styles that were fused into a multifaceted style. As we work our way through the resources of the string quartet, we shall learn that there is no single referential quartet sonority, nothing analogous to the arpeggiated chord or Alberti bass supporting a lyrical melody, which figures so prominently in mid-eighteenth-century keyboard music. Rather, it is the juxtaposition of a large number of possible sonorities that gives the quartet its textural interest, creates the feeling of "conversation among four intelligent people," and contributes to the definition of musical form. As a general rule, listeners and players alike feel most comfortable with quartets whose textures are constantly shifting.

SYMPHONY AND TRIO SONATA

Probably the most important antecedents of the string quartet are the trio sonata and the symphony. Unlike the quartet, neither genre is scoring-specific;

nevertheless, the melodic parts of the trio sonata were, when specified, most often assigned to violins, while the instruments central to the early symphony are the strings. The close relationship between symphony and quartet is attested by several factors in the development of the quartet. The symphony was, in its early stages, a work for string orchestra and, moreover, one that grew from a three-part to a four-part texture, that is, from a piece whose scoring was congruent with that of the trio sonata (two violins plus bass) to a four-part composition with a fully written out viola part. The decline of the continuo, the keyboard accompaniment to this string texture, is coincident with the rise of the viola part. In addition, the performance of symphonies in the eighteenth century favored an alternation of solo and tutti scoring, after the manner of the concerto grosso and usually in accordance with dynamic markings (tutti = *forte*, solo = *piano*); in this sense, the symphony embraced the string quartet: its passages that call for solo performance are, in effect, string quartet textures.[2]

To disentangle the influences of the trio sonata and the symphony on the early quartet is difficult, since in both symphony and quartet the viola was the newcomer to an established texture. Dependence on the bass line, either by its doubling the bass at pitch or an octave higher or by playing repeated notes in the same rhythmic pattern (e.g., repeated eighth notes), is as much a characteristic of the viola part of the early quartet as it is of the mid-century symphony. A glance at almost any early Haydn symphony shows that the number of independent parts operating in a given texture may vary, and this variability is not necessarily the result of a change in instrumentation. That is, all the parts may be truly independent; or they may all be playing in unison or octaves with one another, or some but not all parts may be playing in unison or octaves. The string quartet follows this pattern: the contrast between the simple and vigorous, on the one hand, and the delicate and complex, on the other, is one of the most important means of structuring phrases in early quartets and remains an enduring feature of the genre. Usually dynamic markings reinforce this contrast, but sometimes the subtleties in the texture preclude a simple opposition of loud and soft.

In the prevailing three-part texture in the first minuet of Op. 1, No. 1 (see Example 1.1), the subservience of the second violin to the first, apart from its guest appearance as the bass in bars 15–18, shows Haydn leaning towards the sonorities of orchestral music. But there are movements from the early quartets in which Haydn appropriates the trio sonata as a chamber texture, with the two upper parts closer to equal thematic stature above a continuo bass: both violins are melodic soloists, while the viola and cello take the place of a *basso continuo* before "progress" is made towards four independent parts.

The opening Adagio of Op. 1, No. 3, a sonata form without the customary repeat signs that divide the movement into two sections, begins with an eight-bar solo for the first violin that is answered at the lower octave by the second violin; the overlap between the two violin solos is given in Example 2.2a. The modulation introduces a new theme, played by the two violins in canon (Example 2.2b). With the imminent arrival on the dominant, the violins are assigned different though equally important material, and the viola begins to sever its links with the cello, eventually to join the first violin in parallel tenths (Example 2.2c). After a violin solo and a conventional trio (violins in thirds above the bass), the exposition closes in four-part texture, with the inner parts animating the rhythm on the first beat of the bar (Example 2.2d).

Example 2.2 Op. 1, No. 3, i, (a) bars 7–11

(b) Bars 15–16

(c) Bars 20–22

(d) Bars 31–33

A similar instance of trio sonata is provided by the central Adagio ma non tanto from Op. 1, No. 4 (see Example 2.3), in which the coequal status of the upper parts is aided by a change of timbre for the second violin—*con sordino*—and by having it repeat the ends of the first violin's melodic utterances an octave lower in the manner of an off-stage echo.[3] The trio sonata parody is heightened by the walking character of the bass part and the rhythmic congruence of viola and bass for most of the movement.

As in the Adagio from Op. 1, No. 3, the relationship between the upper parts is fluid: the echo becomes stylized as the piece moves from opening theme to second group to development. The initial exchange establishes a standard relationship between the violins, the echo filling out the first violin's rest (Example 2.3a). As this part becomes more fragmented, the violins play against each other at closer range, then combine quasi-canonically at a quarter-note's distance to produce a harmonic sequence in a more conventional trio texture. (When this distance is reduced to an eighth note, the second violin no longer duplicates the first exactly.) The outlet of the tension created by the ever closer proximity of the two violins—an echo in the lower string parts heightens this tension—is a cadenza-like flourish for the first, warbling at the top of its register; the second's dutiful imitation concludes the exposition (Example 2.3b).

The second part of the movement, an extract of which is given in Example 2.3c, introduces a new inner-part pairing and antiphonal opposition between the first violin and the three lower strings. The original echo effect is now, amusingly, extended to four-part chords. The movement returns to C major with an exact canon for the violins (Example 2.3d): attention on the upper voices is focused, and intensified, by a suspension of activity in the lower parts: thus the theme and original tonality return together, but the sense of recapitulation is not completed until the lower parts resume their "walking" accompaniment.[4]

Example 2.3 Op. 1, No. 4, iii, (a) bars 1–2

(b) Bars 11–13

(c) Bars 17–22

(d) Bars 29–31

This Adagio ma non tanto behaves like a trio sonata on two levels. On the one hand, the two upper parts are set against one another over an accompaniment that is for the most part "neutral": the viola and cello rarely get caught up in the interplay between the violins. On the other hand, the violins are usually heard separately (with the second echoing the first), with the result that the viola and cello, though rhythmically aligned, must play different notes in order to produce three-part harmony. To see how fragile their interdependence is, it is instructive to take a closer look at the lower strings at the start of the movement. In the first half-bar, the viola and cello play in tenths and, together with the first violin, create a three-part counterpoint on tonic and dominant harmonies. The required resolution of the lower parts—the cello's g, the viola's b^1—is the same note, C. The cello resumes its steady eighth-note pace with a characteristic octave drop on C, and the viola duly follows in the higher octave (see the brackets in Example 2.3a) before the three-part counterpoint causes their paths to separate once more. The viola's rhythmic allegiance gives the illusion that Haydn is unsure whether it is meant to *follow* the cello or actually to *double* it, and the listener might be puzzled at the ambivalence of the passage. It may not be easy for ears accustomed to the richer quartet textures of the 1780s to hear Haydn's part-writing as unproblematic—the illustration offered here is representative of what happens throughout the early quartets—but it is entirely characteristic for his part-writing to be as dense or as sparse as is necessary to convey the musical message. Seen in this light, the convergence of viola and cello for two notes in the first part—the exposure is heightened by an overall thin texture—is perfectly judged. To have given the viola different notes or allowed it to rest would have called undue attention to a line whose degree of freedom from the bass is a function of the harmony and counterpoint. To disparage such relationships between the parts in Haydn's early string quartets as "primitive" is to underestimate the importance of these controlling factors.

ANTIPHONAL TEXTURES

If the string quartet is, in Goethe's phrase, a conversation among the four players, then it is natural for the players to alternate between coming to the fore and having a supporting role in the musical discourse or being silent altogether. In the Classical period, much music is organized by paired phrases, one responding to the other by repeating the opening phrase or by making a balanced response to it. If, for instance, the opening phrase (the *antecedent*) seems to require an answer because it ends with an inconclusive harmony—most often a dominant—the response (the *consequent*) might start with the same material but modify the continuation so as to end on the tonic, or it might modulate to a new key altogether.

Putting together the notion of conversation and the principle of antecedent-plus-consequent phrase construction, we often find in chamber music that a musical idea is stated twice, with prominence given to different instruments in the two phrases. If the piece is scored for an ensemble of mixed timbre, say, a quartet for piano and strings, then the ensemble can divide into groups to highlight the differences in timbre. In the final movement of his Piano Quartet in G Minor, K. 478, for instance, Mozart presents most of the themes twice, once with the piano as the leading (or solo) instrument, once with the string players. The deployment of the transition theme, shown in Example 2.4, is typical of this procedure. An eight-bar phrase assigned to the piano arrives on a D major chord, the dominant of G. The strings take over, beginning their consequent phrase with an almost exact repeat of the antecedent but ending with a perfect cadence in the *key* of D major.

If the ensemble is homogeneous—the string quartet consists of four instruments of the violin family—the contrast between the conversing groups will be easier to grasp if the antecedent and consequent phrases are set in different octaves. This happens automatically when the viola or cello responds to the first violin, but examples of these pairings are rare before 1780. In the first movement of Mozart's Quartet in G, K. 387, the principal second-group theme, given in Example 2.5, is initially assigned to the second violin, the first violin responding to it six bars later in a higher octave. Since the antecedent is of irregular length—six bars, rather than four or eight—the consequent is extended to eight bars; this extension itself makes use of the antiphonal principle, with the second violin now answering the first at the lower octave (shown by the added brackets). This example has a further twist: the second violin's response is, technically, an inner part, as the first violin soars above it. In other words, Mozart distributes thematic interest across the two violin parts by developing a new idea for the first violin above an echo of an earlier theme.

[Allegro moderato]

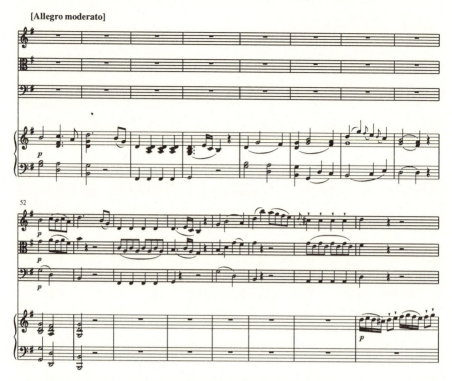

Example 2.4 Mozart, Piano Quartet in G Minor, K. 478, iv, bars 44–59

I have chosen examples by Mozart in the 1780s because the principle of antiphony is clearly laid out in so much of his instrumental music. Not only does his more varied chamber music scoring—piano and string, piano and wind, mixed wind and string ensembles—reflect a preference for antiphonal pairing of phrases, but the later chamber music for homogeneous ensembles continues along these lines, for example, the prominent cello melodies in the "Prussian" string quartets and the soloistic first violin and viola in the string quintets.

Haydn's use of antiphony in the early quartets takes on a number of forms. Sometimes the alternation of pairs of instruments is straightforward enough, the central Presto of Op. 1, No. 3, begins as an exchange of short duets, with each violin paired with one of the lower instruments. Elsewhere, the play between instrumental groups may occupy only part of a phrase, as in the Echo movement from Op. 1, No. 4. The first movement of Op. 1, No. 1, shows the lower strings making quick responses to a violin duet, but these exchanges occur only at the ends of phrases (Example 2.6). In effect, bars 3–4 are a chamber response to an opening orchestral figure, reinforced by the high register of the violins and the change from *forte* to *piano*.

Example 2.5 Mozart, String Quartet in G, K. 387, i, bars 25–38

Example 2.6 Op. 1, No. 1, i, bars 1–4

The first movement of Op. 2, No. 1, includes an early example of Haydn's pitting the inner parts against a soloistic first violin in antiphonal setting. In the closing theme, the active parts are taken by the second violin and viola in thirds below a sustained first-violin e^3; the two-bar motive duly receives its reply when the first violin extends the figure to a four-bar solo with perfect cadence (Example 2.7a). In the exposition there follows an exact repetition of this six-bar passage; in the recapitulation, though, this repetition is both rescored and recomposed, to allow the lowest pair of instruments to participate motivically and the two violins to develop a new, more conclusive sixteenth-note figure (Example 2.7b).

Example 2.7 Op. 2, No. 1, i, (a) bars 22–28

(b) Bars 96–107

STRING QUARTET AS ARIA

It is in the slow movement of Haydn's earliest quartets that the ideals of chamber music appear most often to be betrayed. These pieces are said to bring little musical interest to the lower strings: their accompaniment patterns are predictable and lacking in variety, and fail to interact with the melodic line above them. I refer to this type of texture as "aria" not so much because the style of these movements imitates contemporary music for solo voice and orchestra, but because it favors the first violin almost unremittingly. Being set in a slow tempo and surrounded by shorter, faster movements, these arias dominate many of the quartets in Op. 1 and Op. 2. The Adagio of Op. 1, No. 1, presents such an extremely dull picture of chamber music that even a sympathetic voice like Tovey's mockingly dismissed it as "a poor and pompous specimen of a Neapolitan aria in which the first violin is a tragedy queen singing an appeal to generations of ancestral Caesars."[5] The aria is framed by an introduction in which the second violin is given a share of interest and a postlude that exhibits some textural contrast, but bars 8–35, omitted from Example 2.8, plod along in much the same way as bars 5–7.

Example 2.8 Op. 1, No. 1, iii, (a) bars 1–7

(b) Bars 36–42

There are two slow quartet movements from around 1770 in which the first violin imitates the voice by performing a stylized recitative. Haydn had used a solo violin recitative in one of his early programmatic symphonies, No. 7 (*Le midi*), of 1761, and actually subtitled that part of the slow movement Recitativo. In the introductory Adagio of the slow movement to his quartet Op. 9, No. 2 (see Example 2.9), his technique is subtler: as the brackets in Example 2.9 show, the first violin not only delineates a solo line but contributes much to the broken chord effects—a parody of harpsichord technique, complete with *acciaccature*.

Even more striking are the two recitatives in Op. 17, No. 5, which, unusually, are integrated into the movement rather than serving a preparatory function. Thus they go well beyond the role of parody, representing the transition sections

Example 2.9 Op. 9, No. 2, iii, bars 1–8

Example 2.9 (*cont.*) Op. 9, No. 2, iii, bars 5–8

of a sonata form. The first modulates to the relative major and introduces a lyrical second subject in that key; the second passage, given in Example 2.10, prepares a reworking of this theme, as a closing subject, in the tonic.[6]

Example 2.10 Op. 17, No. 5, iii, bars 46–71

The aria is a familiar *topos* in the string quartet, and as late as Op. 33 Haydn wrote a slow movement—the Larghetto e cantabile of No. 5—in which the lower parts slavishly support a solo violin almost from beginning to end.[7] But from Op. 9 onwards the lower parts of such movements are either more varied or they are integrated into the whole. To be sure, the domination of the quartet by the first violin is difficult to avoid: in a *galant* style, in which melody plus accompaniment is the norm, nothing is gained by a deliberately equal sharing of melodic interest between two violins. As with the quartet as a whole, the accompanying parts in slow movements are interesting so long as their relationship to the principal line remains flexible.

The Adagio of Op. 9, No.1, starts as a siciliano for first violin (Example 2.11a), whose accompaniment gives little hint of the changes that will take place later; even though the theme will be passed briefly to the second violin in bar 5, the basic solo-plus-accompaniment pattern perseveres through the modulation to the second group. As they approach the expected arrival on the dominant, however, the lower strings begin to diverge from their accompaniment pattern. To begin with, the second violin ties some of its repeated notes together to form a dotted quarter note tied to an eighth—see Example 2.11b, at *(a)*—which helps to join bars 16–18 to make a three-bar group. It then introduces a chromatic passing c♯[2] in a push towards cadence in the following bar, at *(b)*; this note takes the place of the eighth-rest caesura in bar 2. The viola supports the chromatic intensification by playing below violin 2 in sixths, at *(c)*, further eroding the siciliano pattern. For the cadence in bar 18, the second violin converts the first solo into a duet in thirds, at *(d)*, but it is the cello that becomes the primary focus of interest, by moving up a step and so diverting the cadence at *(e)*, a dramatic moment that results in the first break in activity heard so far.

Example 2.11 Op. 9, No. 1, iii, (a) bars 1–4

The process is repeated in bars 19–21, with several interesting variants. First, the viola supports the smoother quality of the middle bar with an appoggiatura b♭; by anticipating this at the previous bar *(f)*, the viola aligns itself with the first

Example 2.11 *(cont.)* (b) bars 16–30

violin part. (This b♭ is not only a dissonance, like the first violin g♯^{2} with which it is paired, it clashes with the b-natural grace note that had already been heard in bar 17 and is repeated here.) Now the cello supports the lower strings by moving to f at the beginning of bar 20 and tying it over for five eighths *(g)*, removing virtually all traces of the siciliano.

The cello, having made a deceptive cadence in bar 18, does so again in bar 21 *(h)*. This time the deception is more dramatic: not only is the flattened sixth a surprise, the octave leap (supported by the viola) opens up the low register, thus inviting the inner parts to fill this space and extend the phrase well beyond its expected three-bar limit. The viola starts by picking out the descending line in the first violin's cadential e^2–(f^2–)d^2–c^2. (The alteration of e^1 to e♭^{1} is required by the cello's A♭: compare *(i)* and *(j)*.) The three-note figure is imitated by the second violin and finally echoed rhythmically by the first.

The tension created by the deceptive harmony and extra motivic activity is gradually released over the next five bars. When the first violin regains its prominence, it is accompanied not by a resumption of the siciliano pattern but by strong, single chords whose rhythmic reversal at *(k)* dramatically sets up the final climax and cadence in bars 26–28. The section ends with the inner parts initiating the dialogue with the first violin melody *(l)*, and the cello joins in at the final bar *(m)*.[8]

I have dwelt at length on the Adagio of Op. 9 No.1, because it illustrates that the parts of a quartet may interact with one another without necessarily sharing the same material: an accompaniment can be imaginative without contributing to thematic development.

MESSA DI VOCE

One technique by which Haydn is able to integrate melody and accompaniment in aria-like slow movements is to have the inner parts begin the action underneath a held note in the first violin. An early example of this occurs in the Adagio of Op. 9, No. 6 (Example 2.12). The initial five-note accompaniment figure, comprising repeated notes and a slurred stepwise descent, is developed in a number of ways. It provides material for the continuation of the solo violin part at *(a)*, after the initial held note. Its slurred triplets provide new lyrical impetus for the violin solo at *(b)*, while its repeated notes animate the accompaniment during the transition to the dominant, at *(c)*. The imminent cadence on the dominant is heightened by the return of the original figure in three upper parts at *(d)*; the cadence is delayed by four bars by the cello's diversion to g♯. That it is the cello alone, and not the quartet as a whole, that is responsible for the deceptive cadence at *(e)* is underscored by the triplet motive passing into the cello part: since this motive begins with a rest, the outcome of the cadence isn't known until *after* the downbeat of bar 16, that is, after the other instruments have contributed their notes to the expected B major chord.

The foregoing example shows another feature that Haydn has borrowed from the world of singing, the long-held note in the solo part, underneath which a more active inner or bass part gains the listener's attention. In slow music, violinists normally begin such notes quietly, reaching full volume some time after the initial attack; this practice is closely related to the *messa di voce* in vocal technique, whereby a long note begins quietly, crescendos to a climax, and finishes with a decrescendo.[9]

The advantage of giving the first violin a high, held note is that it partly deflects interest towards the other instruments: the second violin can play the tune underneath, with the viola taking full responsibility for the inner part (by offering,

Example 2.12 Op. 9, No. 6, iii, bars 1–20

for example, support in thirds or sixths). Though the first-violin *messa di voce* is deployed with great effect at the beginnings of other Haydn slow movements, the principle can be applied at any tempo and at any point in a movement.

At the beginning of the Presto finale from Op. 17, No.5, given as Example

2.13a, the viola and cello are competing for ownership of the bass part. The conflict between them is resolved when the first violin takes a high g^2 and pushes the violin duet into the inner parts (Example 2.13b). With the viola now occupied with second-violin music, the cello alone is responsible for the bass.

Example 2.13 Op. 17, No. 5, iv, (a) bars 1–4

(b) Bars 20–25

The first violin need not literally hold on to the note, in a singing manner: repetitions and other forms of embellishment are also possible. In another Presto finale from Op. 17, No. 1 in E major, both violins sustain an E, beneath which the viola and cello develop the opening theme of the movement (Example 2.14a). The repeated E's not only complement the lower parts rhythmically, they also anticipate the ensuing eighth-note accompaniment pattern. In the development, Haydn deploys a similar arrangement of the parts. This time, however, the cello is called upon to screw up the harmonic tension, with V–I to F♯ major and later to G♯ major. As can be seen from Example 2.14b, the first violin alone takes the held note, leaving the thematic development to the inner parts.

Example 2.14 Op. 17, No. 1, iv, (a) bars 12–22

(b) Bars 103–108

UNISON WRITING

Despite the premium that writers have placed upon part-writing in the string quartet, it cannot be denied that many of the best effects occur when the quartet is playing in unison. If versatility is a fundamental attribute of the genre—and, as we have seen, the quartet can emulate the symphony and the concert aria as well as act as a chamber ensemble—then unison writing can provide highly effective contrast both to rich four-part sonorities and to the lighter textures created when two instruments share a line. As we saw in Example 2.6 above, the unison opening of Op. 1, No. 1, creates the atmosphere of the symphony, as a foil to the upper two or lower three strings on their own. Paradoxically, we perceive the responses as lighter, because the dynamic is quieter and because fewer instruments are playing, though the unison texture is in a technical sense the lightest since it consists of just one "part."[10]

Not all unison textures will be perceived as symphonic: some will give the impression that the four parts have agreed to speak *as a quartet* in one voice, either to allow a single voice to refract into four-part harmony (as in the opening bars of Op. 20, No. 4, in D major), or to show solidarity by making a rhetorical gesture. Perhaps the most striking of these rhetorical unisons are found in the slow movement of Op. 20, No. 2, in C major; there are also examples in the recitative passages of Op. 17, No. 5 (see Example 2.10), and in the slow movement of Op. 9, No. 3, in which a brief outburst in unison triplets enables Haydn to transfer the moving part smoothly from one outer voice to the other (Example 2.15).

Example 2.15 Op. 9, No. 3, iii, bars 24–26

COMPLEX COUNTERPOINT, CHROMATIC HARMONIES

At the opposite end of the spectrum to unison writing, composers can create the impression that the parts of a quartet are equally important because they all contribute to a contrapuntal or harmonic complexity that is audible on the surface of the music. Rigorous counterpoint is a special feature of the three fugal finales of Op. 20, which will be discussed in the following chapter; nothing in Opp. 1, 2, 9, or 17 approaches the contrapuntal writing in these finales.

Perhaps the most striking example of harmonic complexity in the string quartet before 1785 is the coda to the first movement of Op. 20, No. 5, which pushes the tonality far from the home key when the listener most expects tonal confirmation. The passage, which will be discussed in greater detail in chapter 4, is also striking because it is not based on a tune: it is, in a sense, pure part writing, the quartet exploring the deepest regions of F minor without the benefit of a thematic map, so to speak. Though nothing so powerful exists in the earlier quartets, hints of this procedure—brief passages in which time appears to stand still—are found occasionally in Op. 9 and Op. 17 first movements. In the transition to the relative major in the first movement of Op. 9, No. 4 (Example 2.16), interest is focused on the second violin's chromatic shift and the cello's slippage from A to G; a bar later, Haydn is firmly established in the second group.

Example 2.16 Op. 9, No. 4, i, bars 15–17

A more extended passage of harmonic saturation in a neutral thematic setting occurs in the first movement of Op. 17, No. 2, at bars 32–33 (see Example 2.17a). The expected cadence in C major in bar 29, forecast by first-violin bravura and especially by the activity of the inner parts at *(a)*, is interrupted not by the conventional submediant but by a diminished chord, at *(b)*, which supports an extension of the violin solo during the next three bars. There now follows a short, nonthematic passage initiated by the same chord to which an e^1 has been added, which resolves as a "normal" deceptive cadence at *(c)*. The resumption of activity is marked by a short-circuiting to a previous point in the music (compare *(a)* and *(d)*). In the development section (Example 2.17b), where the passage in question is extended to four bars, the equal importance of the four parts is guaranteed by the downward chromatic slippage through three diminished seventh chords.

Example 2.17 Op. 17, No. 2, i, (a) bars 26–38

(b) Bars 63–67

So far I have been discussing techniques that might be applied to almost any mid-18th-century instrumental piece. I shall turn now to aspects of composition that are associated more specifically with string instruments in general, and the quartet in particular.

CELLO AS MELODIC LINE

If the string quartet developed in large measure from the symphony and chamber music with a *basso continuo*, then the natural role for the cello is to take the bass part. But there is a crucial difference between the two genres: in the symphony the bass is scored for a multiple of instruments, including cello and double bass; in that scoring, its interaction with the upper parts is limited both by the flexibility of the double bass and the registral space separating it from the upper strings. Once the solo cello is freed from the continuo, or from a larger section of bass instruments, it can take on new roles in chamber music. (The most striking, and historically famous, of these is its melodic role in Mozart's three late quartets written for the cello-playing king of Prussia and in the two string quintets that are contemporary with them.)

That the cello parts in Haydn's quartets continue to behave like the bass parts of symphonies and trio sonatas has been amply documented in the literature; indeed, the scoring of the bass part in his earliest quartets was for a long time disputed.[11] Haydn seems aware of the potential of the soloistically scored bass part in his earliest quartets, and he begins to exploit it more consistently from Op. 9 onwards. But the enduring popularity of the "Prussian" quartets and of Mozart's later chamber music generally has overshadowed the fact that it was the older composer who first gave the cello a melodic role in the string quartet texture and, crucially, created a highly varied set of roles to bridge the extremes of melody and bass. In other words, in Haydn's quartets we find the cello fulfilling a "neutral" continuo role, or interacting motivically with the upper parts, or having sufficiently distinctive melodic characteristics that it is accompanied from above.

Brief cello melodies in a high register, which must be accompanied from below and thus require the viola to assume the bass part, appear in Haydn's Op. 20 quartets and will be considered in later chapters. The first full-length tune for the cello in a high register is the opening eight bars of the variations from the third quartet of Op. 50, a set roughly contemporary with Mozart's "Prussian" quartets and dedicated to the same cello-playing king.[12] Of greater interest to the quartet as an integrated ensemble of soloists, however, are passages in which the cello part dominates in its own register, accompanied from above.

A comparison of the trio sections of the D major quartets from Op. 20 and Op. 33 offers a glimpse of the evolution of low-register melodic cello writing. In the earlier movement (Example 2.18a) the cello theme comprises a string of eighth notes that join the roots of a I–IV–V–I progression in the home key, followed by a similar progression in the dominant. The equivalent passage from the later quartet (Example 2.18b) is based on the same harmonic progression, but now with a rhythmic profile that distinguishes clearly between upbeat and downbeat and, as a result, lends itself to a more varied use of the other instruments in the second half of the trio.

Example 2.18 (a) Op. 20, No. 6, iii, bars 21–28

(b) Op. 33, No. 6, iii, bars 27–34

The regularity of the passages illustrated in Example 2.18 is partly a function of their position; trio sections are as a rule simpler, more regularly constructed. At times, though, Haydn allows the cello to begin thematically in a low register only to retreat to its standard position of bass line. The Menuet of Op. 64, No. 1, in C major begins as a cello solo (see Example 2.19), but at both the diversion to A minor at bar 4 and the full cadence in bar 8 the cello takes the bass line, allowing the first violin to assume the melodic line for the phrase endings. It is important to recognize that Haydn is not passing a single idea between the two instruments, but rather that one melodic line ends prematurely while another emerges from an accompanying part.

Menuet

Example 2.19 Op. 64, No. 1, ii, bars 1–8

REGISTRAL SPACE

If the cello part of the early quartet represents a transitional phase between a Baroque continuo and a line that is thematically and texturally integrated in the ensemble, then it becomes instructive to study these parts in terms of the register they occupy. The lowest part of the first ten quartets rarely goes below F; the bottom C towards the end of the slow movement of Op. 2, No. 4, is exceptional, and has been adduced as evidence of the greater effectiveness of cello (compared to the double bass) on the lowest part.[13]

The deep tone of the C string is something that Haydn begins to explore in the late 1760s. The slow movement of Op. 9, No. 5 (Example 2.20), shows a number of ways in which the cello part develops, often with important consequences for the other instruments. The movement opens with a chorale-like texture in close position (see *(a)*); this itself shows a special role for the cello, avoiding a walking bass or the accentuation of strong beats. (Haydn shows a preference for flat keys when using the cello as the bass of a chorale: other examples include the slow movements of Op. 17, No. 4, also in E-flat, and Op. 17, No. 3, in A-flat.) The theme is repeated, at *(b)*, but now the cello drops down to the C string, and so expands the space between the outer parts by an octave. At first, the change seems attributable more to a desire for variation between two statements of the same theme, as the cello returns to its normal register two bars later. But it dips again at *(c)*, in response to the first violin reaching its climax. With the second violin pushing hard against the first, the viola is left in the middle of a registral chasm spanning more than three octaves.

After the imperfect cadence two bars later, at *(d)*, the cello executes one of its characteristic figures joining two phrases. This figure begins, however, in a higher register than we have heard before, and so invites a response from other instruments. In the passage that follows, the first violin embellishes f^2, and the second violin accepts the invitation for dialogue with the cello (with support

Example 2.20 Op. 9, No. 5, iii, bars 1–34

Example 2.20 (*cont.*) Op. 9, No. 5, iii, bars 1–34

from the viola two bars later). The joining figure forms a countertheme to a new first violin melody at *(e)*, and is extended to a full bar of sixteenth notes as the music approaches a provisional cadence in the dominant, at *(f)*. The new violin solo at *(g)* develops the first four notes of the joining figure with rhythmic embellishments; at *(h)* this is reduced to just two notes. At its climax the violin is accompanied by the joining figure played by the lower parts in a rhetorical unison that sets up the cadential six-four chord. The cello, rather than resolving at *(i)* as expected, initiates a closing passage based on the same joining figure—the eighth rest on the downbeat of bar 30 is crucial—to which the first violin responds in alternate bars until the end of the section. Of special interest is the thirty-second-note variation in bar 32, at *(j)*, based on the violin solo seven bars earlier; the first violin duly responds to this with a longer run at *(k)*. Thus the cello, without actually being assigned a melody in the conventional sense, plays a leading role both in motivic development and in defining the relationships among the parts.

STRING-PLAYING TECHNIQUES

Despite the exalted position of the string quartet as a genre of instrumental music and a model of four-part composition, we should not lose sight of the fact that its scoring is highly specific. The composition of idiomatic music for two violins, viola, and cello began at a time when it was accepted, in other forms of chamber music, that alternative instruments might be used in performance, for instance, winds in place of strings and vice versa. It is hard to imagine an early Haydn quartet with, say, a flute taking the first violin part or a bassoon on the bass. That the first violin parts of Classical chamber music were used to illustrate playing techniques in violin tutors is further evidence of the close affinity between compositional material and instrumental technique.[14] The following discussion attempts to classify special features of string writing that we find in some of the early quartets.

Sopra una corda

The prescription to play on one string—by the remark *sopra una corda* or *sull'istessa corda*, or by a long slur drawn over the passage in question—may achieve one of a number of effects. It may highlight the difference between a "bright" upper register and "dark" lower register, for instance, where a theme is played on the same instrument in different octaves (Op. 20, No. 2, beginning and end of the Menuet), or where the composer wishes to highlight the contrast between successive phrases (Op. 33, No. 1, beginning and end of the finale), or in whole sections of a movement: in Op. 20, No. 6, Haydn contrasts the low-register trio with the bright A major sound of the main minuet section by marking all the parts of the trio *sopra una corda*). It can also be used to indicate a *portamento*, or finger slide, between two slurred notes; examples are found in the first movement of Op. 20, No. 3 and, more conspicuously, in the trio sections of the Scherzo of Op. 33, No. 2 and the Menuet of Op. 64, No. 6.

Only one movement before Op. 20 contains an instruction for *sopra una corda*, the Adagio of Op. 17, No. 2. Here the first violin is in dialogue with itself for the first 22 bars, the contrasting tone colors accentuating the presentations of thematic material alternately in high and low registers. In this way Haydn achieves a broad antiphonal design from the resources of a single instrument, making the movement's aria qualities stand out in even greater contrast to the more dialogued textures of the surrounding faster movements.

Double stops

In chamber music, where clarity of part-writing is an important goal, double or multiple stopping is associated mainly with the emphasis of single chords, in conjunction with (or in place of) such markings as *sf, fz, fp*, or simply *f*; examples of this are numerous from Haydn's earliest quartets onwards. Indeed, it is hard to imagine extended use of double stops in the early quartets, given their ancestry in the trio sonata and string symphony. Among the first ten quartets, the only examples of passages of double stopping are found in the Adagio from Op. 2, No. 2. The longest of these, given in Example 2.21, shows three ways in which double stops may be used in the first violin: in imitation of two string parts, to create an antiphonal effect of a duet against the inner parts, as at *(a)*; as a virtuoso effect, with the first violin giving the illusion of taking over the second-violin part, as at *(b)*;[15] and to increase the overall sonority by the addition of a fifth part, as at *(c)*.

Example 2.21 Op. 2, No. 2, iii, bars 25–28

These techniques are found also among passages of double stopping in about half a dozen movements from Op. 9 and Op. 17. Sometimes Haydn uses first-violin double stops to keep all the moving parts of the texture on violins. In the Trio from Op. 9, No. 4, a consistent three-part texture is achieved as a violin duet and thus teases the listeners—including the violist!—about the title of the section. In the Adagio of Op. 17, No. 4, a movement that follows C. P. E. Bach's formal type of "sonata with varied reprise," the varied repeat at bar 11 consists, in effect, of an extra violin part (compare Examples 2.22a and b). It is not that Haydn wishes to deny the viola an interesting role, but rather that he creates an element of expectation by holding the viola and cello in reserve: they are strategically effective when they do have important roles in the thematic development, at bars 21, 54, and 71.

Example 2.22 Op. 17, No. 4, iii, (a) bars 11–14

(b) Bars 44–47

Pizzicato

Pizzicato markings occur in six movements from the ten early quartets, and in two distinctive places in Op. 33, but in none of the eighteen quartets of 1769–72. The gap marks a change of approach to the use of *pizzicato*: whereas the Op. 33 examples forecast a more gestural approach aimed at a rhetorical effect, the early instances emphasize the first violin as the soloist of a serenade, accentuating the distinction between theme and accompaniment.

The central Adagio of Op. 1, No. 6, provides the most clear-cut example of *pizzicato* as a sign for accompaniment, with the three lower parts imitating a plucked string instrument (guitar or mandolin) and thus forming the backing for a solo violin serenade. Less extreme are the trios of the two minuet movements from Op. 2, No. 1; these are also cast as serenades, though here only the viola and cello are marked *pizzicato* (the second-violin figuration is too fast to be plucked), and in the second trio the solo violin briefly joins in the *pizzicato*. And in the trio of the first minuet from Op. 1, No. 3, Haydn incorporates a left-hand *pizzicato* into the first violin part; as with double stops, this is a virtuoso trick, creating the illusion of two instruments playing together.

In the trio section to the first minuet movement from Op. 1, No. 1, the violins respond with *pizzicato* broken chords to bowed gestures from the viola and cello (Example 2.23a); the difference in sound production enhances contrasts of register and shape (short conjunct lines versus longer arpeggiated chords). The two groups interact thematically in the middle of the movement, but the final cadence phrase preserves their functional distinction (Example 2.23b).

Example 2.23 Op. 1, No. 1, ii, (a) bars 35–42

(b) Bars 59–62

Pizzicato on all four instruments creates a sense of equality between all four players: for even though the first violin retains the highest voice in the texture, the playing technique denies it a *bel canto* line—indeed, stopped notes on the violin E string have the shortest reverberation time of any in the ensemble. The *pizzicato* passages in the Adagio of Op. 1, No. 2, punctuate a movement that is in all other respects a violin solo; in this respect they look ahead to the two movements from Op. 33 whose concluding *pizzicato* passages for all four players make movements dominated by the first violin seem to evaporate into thin air.[16] In Op. 1, No. 2, there are *pizzicato* passages at the close of each of the two halves, and this provides an unexpected bonus: a rhetorical unison passage, *coll'arco*, which has the double duty of negating the *pizzicato* and preparing the resumption of the violin solo.

Example 2.24 Op. 1, No. 2, iii, bars 8–12

Apart from the trio sections of minuets, Haydn avoids *pizzicato* in all stylized dances. Though each set of quartets from Op. 9 to Op. 33 contains a siciliano, the subtly changing relationship between theme and accompaniment in these slow movements (see Example 2.11b for an illustration) is sufficient for Haydn to resist the temptation to turn these pieces into serenades.

Open strings

The use of open strings in string quartets is generally undervalued. For one thing, notes to be played on open strings do not easily stand out in the score, except in passages with double stops. Though there is a special "fingering" for open strings, namely, the number 0, Classical composers rarely prescribed it, and the open C of the viola and cello, along with the open G of the violins, need not be specially marked because there is no other way of playing these notes. Secondly, string players have been taught for more than two centuries to use open strings sparingly, and to avoid them whenever possible in exposed solos.[17] Finally, the idea of a limited number of notes with special timbral properties is at odds with the notion of the quartet as the perfect instrumental medium of four-part harmony and counterpoint: that these notes are, moreover, scattered across the range of the instrument, rather than being bunched together in a single register, accentuates the timbral unevenness of the medium.

The principal reasons for which composers have implied, or gone so far as to prescribe, the use of open strings in chamber music are bound up with their greater resonance. In a medium that is by nature intimate—a small number of instruments capable of producing only a moderately loud sound—open strings, especially the lower strings of the deeper instruments, add an extra dimension to the volume produced. Chords made from combinations of open and stopped strings are frequent in the early quartets, and melodic lines joined by a "drone" on an adjacent open string are already found in the first movement of Op. 9, No. 1, in C and Op. 9, No. 3, in G. In these examples, the open strings increase the number of sounding parts, and hence create a more extrovert sound world for the quartet as a whole. Elsewhere, and especially in passages in the key of F, the inclusion of the cello's open C in the dominant chord can contribute to the drama of a passage by enhancing the expected arrival of the tonic. It is worth preserving a distinction between the "extrovert" and the "dramatic" aspects of open strings in chamber music.[18]

The higher open strings of the violin can add brilliance to solo parts, either by being used in the actual rendering or by resonating sympathetically with stopped notes of the same pitch or with one of the overtones. In each of his first four sets of quartets, Haydn wrote one of the six opening movements in a key conducive to such sympathetic vibrations (A major or D major) and in dancelike meter (e.g., a Presto 6/8 instead of the more usual Moderato or Allegro moderato in common time), thereby giving an air of virtuoso brilliance to the first-violin part. In Op. 9, No. 6, for instance, the repeated first-violin E's of the opening theme (Example 2.25a) will probably be played on the A string with the second finger; the open E string will vibrate sympathetically with it. In a later passage, the player will almost certainly use the open E string, which, in the faster pacing of sixteenth notes, will sound especially brilliant (Example 2.25b). That is not to say that the entire movement will sound like a violin concerto: the brilliance of the open E string is a resource that Haydn is able to contrast with more intimate scorings for the quartet.

Example 2.25 Op. 9, No. 6, i, (a) bars 1–3

(b) Bars 26–27

A related technique is *bariolage*, the performance of the same pitch on different strings for the sake of a change of tone color; more particularly, the term is applied to the alternation of a stopped and open string at the same pitch. Examples are found in all periods of Haydn's quartet composition. The first violin part of the Trio from Op. 64, No. 4, which Haydn marks in third position and for which he also prescribes numerous open D's and A's, is quoted in its entirety in Baillot's *L'art du violon* of 1834. The rapid alternation of stopped and open A's, slurred in pairs, is the principal theme of the finale of Op. 50, No. 6, and the source of its traditional nickname, "The Frog." An interesting forerunner to Op. 50, No. 6, is the second minuet of Op. 2, No. 2, in which the *bariolage* implied notationally in the principal motive (Example 2.26a) is then "developed" by being transferred to stopped strings and to an accompanying part (Example 2.26b).

Menuet

Example 2.26 Op. 2, No. 2, iv, (a) bars 1–4

(b) Bars 13–16

Con sordino

The marking *con sordino* is found in only two early Haydn quartets. One is the "echo" movement from Op. 1, No. 4, discussed earlier; the other is the *pizzicato*-accompanied Adagio from Op. 1, No. 6. In both pieces, the use of a mute assists Haydn's compositional intention of having one of the violins stand out from the rest of the quartet texture.[19]

"IDEAL" QUARTET TEXTURES AND QUARTET THEMES

If the success of the string quartet lies in the imitation of musical genres and styles and the coordination of a wide range of textures from unison writing to complex fugal counterpoint, then the notion of an "ideal" texture, a quintessential quartet sonority, might seem a contradiction in terms. Nonetheless, most listeners would agree that the quartet is a distinctive medium, and so the question arises: does it have—did it at some point acquire—a texture that is characteristic of itself? Is it merely the sound of the four instruments playing together that identifies the quartet, or is there a particular disposition of the four instruments that we identify with the quartet, rather than regarding it as an imitation of something else?

To help us answer this question, it is useful to look outside the repertory of the quartet, to see if another genre imitates or parodies the quartet. Many of Beethoven's early piano sonatas, for instance, contain passages in which short motives in the treble and bass oppose one another around a steady pulse of repeated notes. The transition section from the finale of his Op. 7 in E♭ major, part of which is given in Example 2.27, suggests a dialogue between cello and violin, with inner string parts, and is representative of a number of similarly designed textures found among the half dozen piano sonatas of the mid-1790s, the principal instrumental works that precede the start of the Op. 18 quartet project.

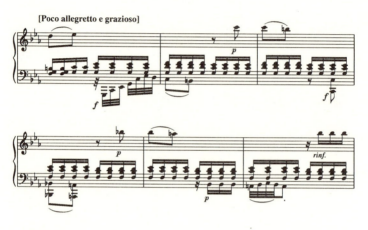

Example 2.27 Beethoven, Piano Sonata in E♭, Op. 7, iv, bars 20–25

Beethoven's last sonata, Op. 111 in C minor, is unusual for presenting three versions of the main theme of the first movement (Example 2.28). Between the rhetorical unison of bars 20–22 and the two-part invention beginning at bar 35 is an arrangement of the theme—given as Example 2.28b—in which the melody ("first violin") is initially accompanied by repeated notes in the inner parts ("second violin, viola") and a simple I–V in the bass ("cello"); the subsequent *portato* notation (*staccato* markings under a slur) is characteristic of violin bowing technique.

Example 2.28 Beethoven, Piano Sonata in C minor, Op. 111, i, (a) bars 20–22

(b) Bars 29–31

(c) Bars 35–37

Compare Example 2.28b with the opening of Haydn's Quartet in E♭, Op. 33, No. 2 (Example 2.29), which exhibits a similar relationship among melody, inner parts and bass. There is no doubt that the first violin is in charge, yet the inner parts are not utterly unrelated to it: what seems a neutral chugging accompaniment complements the melody by filling in the space between the first two notes of the tune. In addition, the melody is presented in a middle register, based on e♭¹, and so does not dominate the ensemble.

Example 2.29 Op. 33, No. 2, i, bars 1–2

The opening of Op. 20, No. 5 (Example 2.30), is similar. Now the pattern of three eighth notes leading to a longer note on a strong beat originates in the lower parts, so that the first-violin rhythm actually begins to grow out of the accompaniment.

Example 2.30 Op. 20, No. 5, i, bars 1–4

If the preceding examples are in some sense typical of the string quartet, they are successful because they promote a kind of equilibrium —melody, inner parts, bass—which in a Classical setting is more satisfactory as a textural point of departure than the outright equality of, say, strict fugue. That texture might move in the direction of greater equality of parts or towards greater domination by the solo violin, but it defines a role for the instruments that may be modified, developed, or negated as the musical argument proceeds.

A final illustration of this type of arrangement, the opening of Op. 76, No. 2, shows an approach to theme that is characteristic of Haydn's later quartets. Example 2.31 shows a perfectly formed four-bar antecedent phrase developed from the opening theme; this will be neatly complemented by a consequent phrase beginning in bar 5 and thus express in its most characteristic terms a harmonic "period." But the motive on which the theme is based, the falling fifth (whence the German nickname "Quinten-Quartett"), is not particularly characteris'.c of the start of melodies; it is an interval that one is more likely to associate with the accompaniment, since each pair of half notes could be the fifth and root of a single chord or the roots of a V–I progression. Indeed, the course of the movement shows this interval moving freely among the four parts.

Example 2.31 Op. 76, No. 2, i, bars 1–4

Quartet themes that are characterized by a simple musical idea—an interval, an ascending or descending neighbor-note figure, a series of repeated notes— lend themselves well to development by all the instruments. And a skillful composer can create an imaginative dialogue by developing figures of this sort, whether they form the opening motive of a theme (as in Op. 76, No. 2) or are prominent in its continuation. In other words, a quartet does not have to begin as a sophisticated dialogue in order to become one.[20]

Table 2.1 presents a list of some quartets by Haydn whose first-movement main themes are based on a single interval or a simple musical pattern:

Table 2.1

First-movement quartet themes by Haydn based on simple opening motives

Quartet	*Characteristic of theme*
Op. 50, No. 1, in B♭	repeated notes
Op. 55, No. 3, in B♭	descending step motion
Op. 64, No. 3, in B♭	upper neighbor-note figure
Op. 71, No. 2, in D	descending leap of an octave
Op. 74, No. 1, in C	double neighbor-note (*nota cambiata*)
Op. 74, No. 2, in F	arpeggiated triad
Op. 76, No. 2, in D minor	descending leap of a fifth

Finally, Haydn devised a special quartet texture that approaches the equal status of parts, by grouping them in pairs playing in parallel thirds, sixths, or tenths. The end of the theme of the finale of Op. 71, No. 1 (Example 2.32a), shows the violins paired in eighth notes accompanied by the viola and cello in sixteenths; the development includes a much longer passage (see Example 2.32b) in which the pairs are opposed in contrary motion in a uniform rhythm.

Example 2.32 Op. 71, No. 1, iv, (a) bars 9–12

(b) Bars 105–114

Such groupings seem a natural thing for four string instruments, but they depend on the cello being capable of playing fluently in a middle register. In most instances, the instruments are set apart antiphonally, that is, with one pair imitating the other. It is crucial, though, for the two pairs to overlap, and thus create the illusion that the bass has dropped out, almost as if the upper parts of two trio sonata ensembles were engaged in combat. The frequent pairings in thirds from Haydn's Op. 20 onwards is a reflection of the cello having attained greater stature in the ensemble in 1772. The first movement of Op. 20, No. 2, which will be analysed in chapter 6, marks the beginning of a long history of a texture whose use extends to the late quartets of Beethoven, and beyond, and merits a study in itself.

The foregoing discussion has focused mainly on the quartets of Opp. 1, 2, 9, and 17. I hope to have shown that these are sophisticated works deserving of attentive listening and careful study. The last six chapters are devoted to the six quartets of Op. 20, which mark the end of three years' intensive engagement with the genre. These works will be discussed in the order in which Haydn evidently wanted them to be arranged, an order that differs from the numbering traditionally assigned to them.[21] Before we look at them individually, we shall consider one more textural resource—fugue—whose significance for Op. 20 and Haydn's subsequent quartet output cannot be underestimated.

3

Fugue

Fugue is the great temptress of the string quartet. It guarantees all the instruments an equal share in the thematic argument, and so offers the first violin an invitation to step off its solo pedestal. In the long term, however, its effect is harmful to the quartet texture: it makes it difficult for the instruments to contribute to the ensemble in an imaginative way, since they all have a roughly equal share of the principal and secondary themes. The string quartet celebrates the diversity of function of its constituent parts; fugue, when practised rigorously, kills off that diversity. Mozart and Beethoven were perfectly aware of the dangers of fugue when, in homage to Haydn, they composed the Molto allegro of K. 387 and the Allegro molto of Op. 59, No. 3, respectively. Neither movement is actually called a fugue, and both begin to abandon the artifice of strict counterpoint immediately after the exposition of the four voices, favoring the more familiar *galant* idiom in a sonata form.

Much the same can be said of Haydn's own essays in fugue, whether they are actually finales labelled "Fuga" or parts of movements whose overall design is based on a different form type (for instance, the development section of a sonata or the conclusion of a variation set). True, some of Haydn's official quartet fugues maintain their contrapuntal artifice longer than others; but sooner or later they yield to homophony. Nevertheless, the concentration of fugues in Op. 20, together with their importance both for the fugal finale as a genre and for fugal texture as a resource of quartet composition, makes a separate study of fugue appropriate to an investigation of Haydn's quartets to 1772.

Since half the Op. 20 finales are fugal finales, fugue has often been seen as the decisive characteristic of the set. Some see it as a way for Haydn to escape the problems of part-writing for four solo instruments in a contemporary style or his less than ideal solution to these problems.[1] Others see it as an important resource of the string quartet, one whose position at the start of the final movement is, moreover, strategic for holding a multimovement piece together. In identifying fugue with Op. 20, historians have accorded much significance to Haydn's preferred ordering of the quartets within the set: 5, 6, 2, 3, 4, 1; the quartets with fugal finales come first, arranged according to the number of subjects presented in the exposition. Op. 20 may be viewed as the product of two subcycles of three quartets, the first subcycle being based on the idea of the fugal finale as practised in the 1760s and with pedagogical traditions of fugue reaching back further.[2]

Commentators have been willing to generalize about Haydn's fugues without subjecting them to a thorough, detailed analysis. Thus we read that "the one in Op. 20/5 [in F minor] is contrapuntally the most ingenious of Haydn's fugues,"[3] or that "the level of contrapuntal artifice in its fugue [Op. 20, No. 6, in A major] is nearly as high as in that in F minor,"[4] or even that "the main theme [of Op.20, No. 2, in C major] no longer has much to do with academic fugue tradition."[5] Of course, we always rely on our impressions in making judgements: no purportedly objective analysis ever dispenses entirely with intuition. Still, a closer reading and comparison of these fugues may help us to rethink, or reformulate, our impressions of them.

There is, of course, a difficulty in writing about fugues in the Classical period, namely, that the theory of *fugue* can tell us little about the overall design of *a fugue* with a beginning, middle, and end; as Tovey so often stressed, fugue is a texture, not a form. Things called "fugue" can begin with intricate counterpoint without maintaining a learned style throughout; conversely, many of Haydn's quartet movements not called "fugue" nevertheless suddenly break into fugal texture, be it a first movement in sonata form (Op. 64, No. 6), a rondo finale (Op. 55, No. 1; Op. 64, No. 5; Op. 71, No. 3), or a variation set (Op. 76, No. 6). The terminology of fugal theory—subject and answer, *stretto* and inversion (*al rovescio*)—cannot help us much with questions of large-scale organization; even the terms "exposition" and "episode" are, as we shall see, insufficient to describe extended passages as formal components. The study of fugues must be twofold, one that takes account both of structure in the large and of texture in the small.[6]

If Mozart and Beethoven composed their quartet fugues in homage to Haydn as the first master of the fugal finale, Haydn's own fugues are a part of the mid-eighteenth-century tradition of instrumental fugal composition: they are the survivors of that tradition. Viewed contrapuntally, Haydn's fugues are not "modern": he does not integrate the techniques of fugal writing and the *galant* style simultaneously as, for instance, Mozart does with his regular four-bar groupings in K. 387. Rather, the old and the new are placed side by side; integration is a "horizontal" process, the reconciliation of the learned and the *galant* by juxtaposition, not superposition.

We can see this in the treatment of his themes. The principal subjects of all three fugues are substantial themes comprising a number of distinct ideas; more particularly, their irregular phrase organization makes the process of the fugal exposition sound learned: the subject of the F minor fugue is six bars long, divided 4+2; that of the A major fugue is four bars, but divided 1+3; while the subject of the C major, thought to be the most modern of the three fugues, is 3½ bars long with no clear rhythmic or motivic point of division. These metric irregularities are what drive Haydn's fugal expositions forward, without recourse to antecedent–consequent phrase building. But in the course of two of the fugues—the F minor and C major—the subject is reduced to its head-motive. These short, characteristic figures not only make it easier for the various parts to respond to each other—flexibly, as befits the parts of a quartet—but also facilitate a regular rhythm, with exchanges of 1+1 or 2+2. When, fifteen years later, Haydn wrote another fugal finale—which was to be his last—he had dispensed with the artifice of multiple subjects: the finale of Op. 50, No. 4, has a two-bar subject, which can generate four- and eight-bar phrases without recourse to abbreviation.

Though all three finales begin in the manner of a double fugue, that is, a fugue in which a pair of lines is initially presented as a two-part counterpoint, it is easy to identify one of these as the principal subject: it spans the entire unit space in which the fugal material is presented and has strong motivic features. The accompanying line is either shorter (in the F minor fugue), less sharply profiled (A major), or both (C major). Although Haydn arranged the first three quartets of Op. 20 according to the number of subjects consistently presented in the expository sections of the final fugues, and subtitled them respectively *a 2 soggetti*, *con 3 soggetti* and *a 4tro soggetti*, it would be wrong to infer a gradual increase in contrapuntal severity from one work to the next. All three are, strictly speaking, double fugues:[7] the discrepancy in the number of additional subjects (or "countersubjects") pretty much vanishes once the opening exposition has run its course. The F minor *fuga a 2 soggetti* is the contrapuntal poor relation of the set only in name: as it runs its course, it integrates motivic ideas that had not been deployed consistently enough in the exposition to be called "subjects." Conversely, two of the subjects of the C major fugue behave more like ordinary inner parts, without participating in the actual fugal development: their status as subjects results simply from their consistent presence in the opening exposition and alongside later statements of the principal subject.

It is customary to make a distinction between an "exposition," in which the subject is presented in full at least once, and an "episode," where the subject is reduced and developed, often by sequential treatment. What we find in Haydn's quartet fugues, though, is that the last statement in an exposition is followed by an unwinding of material, less rigorous in its thematic presentation but not episodic in the narrower sense of implying development by reduction. Rather than calling all the music between two expositions an "episode," I shall use the term "continuation" when referring to these transitional passages between expositions and episodes.

The term "exposition" is itself problematic. All three fugues begin with a substantial paragraph of music in which the four parts enter in turn with the principal subject, alternately on the tonic and dominant, followed by a fifth entry at the same pitch level and in the same instrument as the beginning; these make up the first exposition of fugue. (The fifth entry is sometimes described as a "redundant" entry, since it does not identify a new contrapuntal part; its role here is to provide harmonic closure for an exposition that would have otherwise ended with a dominant statement of the theme, that is, to convert an open-ended I–V–I–V progression based on four entries into a tonally closed I–V–I–V–I.) Subsequent returns of the subject often occur singly; occasionally Haydn presents the subject consecutively at the same pitch level, rather than at the distance of a fifth (as conventional subject and answer). Since it hardly seems adequate to refer to a short section embracing a single entry under the rubric "exposition," I use the term "statement" instead, with "exposition" reserved for longer sections comprising statements of the subject at different pitch levels; these often appear towards the end of the movement with the application of a new fugal technique (*stretto* or inversion).

It is generally accepted that the three fugal finales of Op. 20 are different in character, the seriousness and severity of the F minor contrasting with the lighthearted grace of the A major; in the C major fugue, which concludes the fugal quartets in the set, the *galant* triumphs over the learned. It may, however, be dangerous to read too much into the fugues themselves in these terms; they are, after all, the finales of works whose divergent personality traits have been well established in preceding movements. To a limited extent, in fact, the very fugality of the finales draws these three works closer together rather than emphasizing their differences: they furnish the quartets with grandeur as well as learnedness. The first three movements of the capricious A major quartet are comparatively short, but its substantial, intricate, and carefully wrought finale ensures that its overall impact is not slight. The F minor fugue is generally regarded as the most serious of the three because of its purportedly tragic tone and greater use of contrapuntal artifice, yet the subject itself, which Haydn cribbed from a long-established tradition, has a propensity to be developed in a certain way. Indeed, it would be odd if Haydn had not introduced inversion, *stretto*, and canon into this fugue, and it is unlikely that the discerning eighteenth-century musician would have credited him with these ingenuities, since they inhere in the theme itself.

The discussion of each fugue will focus on points of distinction in their capacity as individual movements. For the sake of simplicity, subjects are identified by roman numbers, their constituent motives by small letters: thus, for example, Ia always designates the "head-motive" of the principal subject.

OP. 20, NO. 5, IN F MINOR

The exposition of this fugue is given as Example 3.1. The principal subject is a familiar *topos* of eighteenth-century fugue, the pattern 5–1–♭6–♯7 (or 5–3–♭6–♯7) with its characteristic drop of a diminished seventh being found, for example, in the subjects of no fewer than three of the twenty-four minor fugues from Bach's *Well-Tempered Clavier*, and its appearance in "And with His Stripes" from Handel's *Messiah*—a four-part chorus in F minor—may have been even better known in Haydn's day. It is a theme that, the chromaticism notwithstanding, begins in an archaic vein with long note values and builds into a sequence of intervals with the potential for canon and *stretto*.

Example 3.1 Op. 20, No. 5, iv, bars 1–22

Taking Haydn's title at face value, we would identify the second subject to be the viola part in bars 3–6, its faster note values and off-the-beat start complementing the austerity of the principal subject. The similarity of contour between the head of the principal subject (Ia) and the tail of the second (IIb) tightens the relationship between the two themes. A fugue "a due soggetti" promises repetition of this two-voice counterpoint, and the answer to subject I in the first violin is duly accompanied by subject II in the second violin. As the tonal answer converts the initial descending fifth of subject I into a fourth, f^2–c^2, the contours of the subjects match one another closely.

But the severity of the beginning is deceptive. The first two statements of the principal subject furnish the only examples of a six-bar contrapuntal unit: in all subsequent presentations this subject is reduced to its head-motive (Ia), while the second subject is accordingly reduced to two bars (IIa). Of course, it is in the nature of Haydn's music to develop, and even if the reduction of the subjects obscures their thematic interrelationship, the overall flow of the fugue results from the interaction of these two characteristic motives. Abbreviating these subjects facilitates four-bar phrase building, of which Haydn takes advantage in the episodes and realizes more fully in the recapitulatory expositions in bars 112–23 and bars 145–60.

Though the resultant phrase organization is tighter, the shortened principal subject highlights an unsolved problem, namely, the harmonization of the angular opening of the head-motive itself. Once bars 1–2 have passed, what motivic material will serve as its counterpoint? To some extent the head-motive itself provides the answer. Viewed from the discipline of fugue, the most economical forms of counterpoint are those that use the same motive, i.e. the techniques of *stretto* and canon (Example 3.2).

Example 3.2 Op. 20, No. 5, iv, (a) bars 112–116

(b) bars 145–149

Contrapuntal artifice, however, is often best reserved for points of arrival in large-scale design: it provides the analogue to recapitulation in sonata form, where an exact restatement of the opening would sound lame. The task facing Haydn earlier in this movement is to create a line that provides a suitable counterpoint and rhythmic complementation for the head-motive, and one that at the same time uses different material from either subject. Since good counterpoint favors imperfect consonances over perfect ones, as their quality remains invariant when the parts are inverted (thirds become sixths, etc.), Haydn comes up with two lines that can be embellished sequentially, as shown schematically in Example 3.3: (a) stepwise ascent and (b) descent by thirds.

(a) ascending step motion   (b) descending thirds

Example 3.3 Harmonization patterns for the principal fugue subject of Op. 20, No. 5

These patterns provide a basis for sequence at the half-note level, as can be seen in the viola in bars 7–9 and bars 19–21, respectively, and both even use the same neighbor figure for sequential treatment. Counterpoints based on these patterns appear in the course of the fugue about as frequently as the head-motive of the second subject.

All of Haydn's counterpoints in this fugue are modified to accommodate new situations. Where the principal head-motive is in the bass, the quarter–eighth–eighth rhythm is accommodated to a different rising line (see Example 3.1, bars 13–14, for an illustration), and the pattern changes elsewhere in the fugue. As the first dominant pedal approaches, Haydn introduces the only instance of *al rovescio* treatment of the subject, more as a way of demonstrating the symmetrical construction of the principal motive about the fifth F–C and its surrounding diminished seventh, E–D♭; a third, accompanying voice is a modified IIa.[8]

Table 3.1

Plan of the finale of the Quartet Op. 20, No. 5

Bar	1	23	36	42
Fugue	exposition	continuation + episode	statement	continuation + episode
Sonata form	first group	transition	second group	development
Key	f		A♭	various
Function	i		III	(X)

The plan of the movement, a summary of which is given in Table 3.1, shows Haydn's respect for keys closely related to F minor. This is a general feature of the fugues; and, as one may surmise, the opposition of tonic and dominant in the expositions limits the usefulness of the dominant itself as a point of tonal arrival; instead, keys that are third-related to the tonic (III and VI) are favored, along with the subdominant and supertonic. After the exposition of the F minor fugue, in which a redundant fifth entry stabilizes the home key, a transitional passage prepares two consecutive statements of the theme in the mediant. The procedure—establishing F minor, modulation, theme in A♭—is suggestive of sonata form, and the further course of the movement follows this in its general outline. In a substantial development, motive IIa and the additional counterpoints feature in a variety of sequences, which culminate in a passage of expectancy comprising a long sequential cello solo (bars 95–102) and a nine-bar dominant pedal. The "recapitulation," beginning in bar 112 after a fermata on a dominant ninth, begins with a *stretto* of the principal subject. Paired entries create a more continuous F minor than the expository alternation of subject (tonic) and answer (dominant) would allow. This section builds to a second dominant pedal, which now supports a three-part *stretto* and closes into a canon between the outer parts. Admittedly, the sonata proportions are distorted: the "second group" lasts only six bars. Yet the development, though much longer, is subdivided into sections with distinct contrapuntal patterns; the largest of these lifts the harmony from the remote G♭ major back to the home key via a series of ascending fifths. The polarity of tonic and dominant in fugue prevents Haydn from considering a sonata model for either of the remaining fugues of Op. 20, as both of these are in major keys; but Op. 50, No. 4, in F♯ minor, has a similar trajectory.[9]

Because of its strong thematic links to the fugal tradition and its parading of the classical techniques of development (*al rovescio*, *stretto*, and canon), the F minor fugue is generally viewed as the severest of the Op. 20 fugal finales. Its counterpoint, however, seems no more intricate than that found in the other two movements: mostly the texture is only three-part, with fast note values (quarters and eighths) in only one of three parts at any given time. (By comparison, the parts in the A major finale seem more interactive; that there is less technical variety has more to do with the design of the principal subject.)

Table 3.1

(*cont.*)

(89)92	112	146	161
al rovescio	*stretto* + continuation	canon	(fugal texture abandoned)
false reprise	recapitulation		coda
f → V/f	f → V/f	f	
i → V pedal	i → V pedal	i	

What also distinguishes the F minor as a serious work is its key and its context: it follows three movements of serious character. In this respect, an association of fugal texture with the minor mode may not be far wide of the mark. Writing on Op. 50, Sutcliffe argues for "a structural association of mode with texture: when Haydn chooses to write a minor-key finale it is quite logical that it too should be polyphonic—in fact, a fugue."[10] His claim is unsubstantiated; indeed, it would appear unsupportable, given that neither fugal theory nor practice discriminated in favor of the minor mode. But there are remarkable similarities between Op. 20, No. 5, and the next (and last) quartet fugal finale, i.e. Op. 50, No. 4, in F♯ minor: the themes share a characteristic interval pattern, and they aspire to sonata form in similar ways. These affinities are directly related to the fugues being composed in minor keys.

OP. 20, NO. 6, IN A MAJOR

The basis of the principal subject of this fugue is no less archetypal than that of the F minor: sequential descent by step, reinforced by 2–3 suspension pattern from below (7–6 from above) by the accompanying second subject. These two subjects (Example 3.4) are thematically related in the simplest possible way: both embrace the descent of an octave in A major.

Example 3.4 Op. 20, No. 6, iv, bars 1–4, first and second violins

Because the principal subject is constructed from a sequence, the other subjects also follow sequential designs, and so the thematic materials used in this fugue are limited. The three fugue subjects are, in fact, based on just four ideas: the motivic components of the principal subject (Ia, Ib, Ic) and the stepwise descent of II. The start of the third subject can be seen to be a lightly embellished version of Ic, with the result that the sequence initiated by IIIa appears to migrate from the first violin to the second (Example 3.5).

Example 3.5 Op. 20, No. 6, iv, bars 5–8

The derivation of IIIa from Ic is clinched in bar 23, where the cello sequence presents the two versions in alternation; it is celebrated a few bars later, when Haydn substitutes IIIa for Ic in the principal subject and continues in sequence with more statements of the motive (see Example 3.6). The interrelations among the three subjects are thus a consequence of the contrapuntal pattern into which they are woven, a series of descending triads in which consecutive fifths are avoided by the application of suspension figures, a classic example of fourth-species Fuxian counterpoint.

Example 3.6 Op. 20, No. 6, iv, bars 33–35, first violin

From a contrapuntal point of view, there remains only one further task, the design of a fourth voice. Often Haydn adds nothing at all to this intricate polyphonic web formed by the three fugue subjects. That is, when the three subjects are heard simultaneously, the fourth part is usually resting (bars 5, 9, 13, 48) or sitting on a pedal point (bar 69). The only places where a moving fourth part is added are in the final entry of the opening exposition (bar 17), where the counterpoint is by definition tested most severely; in the *stretto*, where the additional entry of the principal subject duplicates the essential descending line of subject III (viola and violin 1, bars 66–68); and in the final bars of polyphony (Example 3.7), in which the viola starts in tenths with the cello, then fills the rhythmic gap in the second violin part to make a continuous descending chain of motive IIIa.

Example 3.7 Op. 20, No. 6, iv, bars 88–91

The overall shape of the movement does not offer any particular surprises. The tautness of the exposition makes continuous contrapuntal treatment appropriate; the bass pedal point in 69–75 and the final unison statement are features common to all Haydn's quartet fugues, but are relatively underplayed here. It is possible to discern, however faintly, a slackening of polyphonic rigor from about bar 78, where the use of parallel tenths in the outer parts suggests greater dependence of parts. The same holds for the *al rovescio* passage, in which the pairing of voices in mirror image results in a loss of rhythmic propulsion, with the second and fourth beats of the bar left unarticulated.

As with Op. 20, No. 5, the opening exposition comprises alternating entries on the tonic and dominant, with a fifth, "redundant" entry stabilizing the tonality. The subsequent course of the fugue includes episodes that are thematically and harmonically more exploratory, along with further regions of thematic and tonal stability. At no time is the dominant established in opposition to the home key: as Table 3.2 shows, the E major entry at bar 52 is tonally dependent on the surrounding regions of its relative key, C♯ minor.

When the counterpoint becomes full, Haydn sometimes makes very minor amendments to motives in order to improve sonority, or to avoid an unwanted dissonance or a part-writing solecism. (In bar 23, for instance, the viola's rising pair of sixteenth notes replaces a figure that would have contained an augmented fourth.) But in episodes he transforms the underlying melodic structure of a motive more radically to fit new contrapuntal arrangements. In two passages, IIIa must be extended by a step to accommodate a descending third in the sequential pattern, either by inserting an extra sixteenth note (Example 3.8a) or by enlarging an interior interval (Example 3.8b).

The difference in procedure in Example 3.8 is not fortuitous. The first passage is more episodic in the fugal sense; Haydn explores an unfamiliar harmonic region with a new texture, sixteenth-note runs in parallel tenths. The second, however, is a more tightly knit development of motives—Ia and IIIa are directly juxtaposed for the first time—and so preserves their original rhythms.

Table 3.2

Plan of the finale of the Quartet Op. 20, No. 6

Bar	1	22	25	27	35	37	44
Fugue	exposition (5 entries)	continuation	episode	statement (2 entries)	continuation	episode	statement
Key	A		f♯	D		A	c♯
Function	I		vi	IV		I	iii

If the return to A major in *stretto* at bar 61 (see Example 3.8b) is heard as a recapitulation of the opening, analogous to bars 112 in the F minor fugue, it is greatly understated. Not only do the paired entries of the principal subject overlap with the final development of motives Ia and IIIa, but the harmony has already resolved to A major at the downbeat of bar 61. The dominant pedal

Example 3.8 Op. 20, No. 6, iv, (a) bars 41–43

(b) Bars 56–62

Table 3.2

(cont.)

47	52	57	61	69	80	92
episode	statement	episode	exposition (2 sets *stretto*)	continuation	exposition (2 sets *stretto*)	continuation unison
	E	c♯	A			
	V	iii	I	V pedal → I		

stretched across bars 69–75 would then seem an afterthought, unnecessary to the structure of a movement that had already found its way back to the home key. Its purpose is to prepare for the very slight relaxation in contrapuntal rigor in the final 20 bars: parallel tenths in the outer voices (bars 77–79), loss of rhythmic independence at the start of the *al rovescio* (bars 81–82), and the unison coda.

It would be a mistake, however, to claim that the final page of this fugue has abandoned the polyphonic style. Rather, Haydn has let up briefly, so as to set up the final whirlwind of four-part counterpoint in the penultimate line. The last four bars of the piece, in which the principal subject is developed in unison, may be thought of as a celebration of 91 bars of counterpoint, a musical round of applause by which the quartet congratulates itself—that is, its composer—for sustaining polyphonic texture of such a high order for so long.

OP. 20, NO. 2, IN C MAJOR

If the C major finale seems the most modern of Haydn's quartet fugues, this is probably due to surface features: the chromatic slide in the very opening gesture of the principal subject, the jaunty rhythms of a lively 6/8 tempo, and the preponderance of episodic rather than expository material. The fugue is no less rigorously worked out than its companions in Op. 20, but full statements of its four subjects are widely spaced, and a long passage of homophonic writing dominates the last quarter of the movement. Thus the opposition of tonic and dominant, which is the basic principle of fugal construction, appears to desert the movement at an early stage. The exposition itself, however, is worked out in a thoroughly rigorous manner: its four subjects present themselves with the highest degree of severity.

In common with the other Op. 20 fugues, the exposition begins with two subjects in counterpoint; these are the most prominent themes in the movement, and their constituent parts are motivically related: motives Ia, IIa, and Ic all begin with repeated notes on the weak eighths of the bar (2 and 3, or 5 and 6). The initial octave leap in Ia is also registrally linked to IIa and Ic; it sets in motion the various descending lines that provide the skeleton of this opening theme complex, shown in Example 3.9. Viewed in this way, we can understand the opening counterpoint as a tightly knit set of descending lines that imply a three-part counterpoint with full sonority and strict treatment of a chain of 7–6 suspensions, analogous to the descending lines of the opening of the A major fugue.[11]

Example 3.9 Op. 20, No. 2, iv, (a) bars 1–4

(b) Contrapuntal background to bars 1–4

The other fugue subjects are of lesser importance for the counterpoint. Motive IIIa fills in the counterpoint left "vacant" by II (which had made a late start), while IIIb merely fills out the harmony by adding a third part to the texture. Subject IV is put together from two unrelated ideas, separated by a bar's rest: IVa elaborates the opening of IIIa in a violinistic way (it can usually accommodate string crossing), while IVb is an aimless line that, like IIIb, fleshes out the harmony.

In the opening exposition, the four subjects are rotated in the various instruments. The fourth entry has all four together for the first time, while the fifth, "redundant" entry shows them in tonic position (Example 3.10). The distance between the subjects and their respective answers is 3½ bars, a metrical irregularity that promotes a sense of continuity in the polyphonic fabric.

The primary contrapuntal tension is established by the first two subjects, as shown in Example 3.9 above. For the movement as a whole, however, IVa and the first four notes of IIIa are fundamentally important, since it is these motives that steer the counterpoint from polyphony towards a more *galant*, homophonic style. Motive IIIa is the diatonic counterpart to the chromatic descent in the principal subject, while IVa reinforces this line with parallel thirds and sixteenth-

Example 3.10 Op. 20, No. 2, iv, bars 13–18

note animation. The close relationship between Ia, IIIa, and IVa can be seen clearly in bars 56–57 (Example 3.11a), which anticipate the final section of the movement in which contrapuntal and rhythmic features are teased apart: the run of sixteenth notes now follows the three-voice counterpoint rather than being heard simultaneously (Example 3.11b).

Example 3.11 Op. 20, No. 2, iv, (a) bars 56–57

(b) Bars 129–30

In its overall design, the C major fugue behaves differently from its companions. To begin with, the episodes seem to dominate the form, especially towards the end of the fugue, as a result of Haydn's failure to recapitulate the principal subject when the tonic returns at bars 83, 99, and 124 (129). At comparable

points in the F minor and A major fugues, Haydn marked the return of the home
key with some form of exposition, enhanced by canonic treatment or *stretto*;
here he strikes out instead along new paths. For example, the false entries of the
principal subject in bars 81–82 might well be read as signals for a full-scale
return a bar later, but the harmony spirals upwards, motive Ia rhythmically spin-
ning out of control (Example 3.12). It is only the last return of C major, at bar
152, that brings with it the complete principal subject. After the earlier disap-
pointments, its return here, now with the full complement of subjects, is a welcome event, one that is duly celebrated with a rousing passage in unison.

Example 3.12 Op. 20, No. 2, iv, bars 81–86

Another indication of Haydn's thematic parsimony in the C major fugue is his
reluctance to string together complete statements of the principal subject to form
an exposition. After the opening exposition, complete statements of the principal
subject are presented singly, except for a pair in F major beginning at bar 92. As
one can see from Table 3.3, the statements of the principal subject behave somewhat like a ritornello of a concerto grosso, taking us through a variety of keys
related to C major, but with a tonic recapitulation of the opening withheld until
six bars before the close.

The notion of the fugue subject as ritornello invites us to reassess the form of
the movement as a fugue from beginning to end, albeit with ever longer episodes, ultimately leading to an extended nonfugal passage before the final statement of the subject. That is not to deny that fugal texture breaks down towards

Table 3.3

Plan of the finale of the Quartet Op. 20, No. 2

Bar	1	19	23	29	42	46	49	64
Fugue	exposition (5 entries)	continuation	statement (2 entries)	episode	statement	continuation	episode	statement
Key	C		a		d			e
Function	I		vi		ii			iii

the end the movement and that in the end the *galant* triumphs over the learned style, but rather to suggest that this dualistic viewpoint does not tell the whole story.

THE FUGAL FINALE AS CULMINATION

An important development in instrumental music of the Classical period was the creation of final movements that seem to provide a long-range goal, by being either the end point in a dramatic process spanning the entire piece or a summing up of earlier activity. The string quartet fugue, by progressing from polyphony to homophony, embraces a wide range of styles, and in so doing gives the end of the work greater force. If one compares the fugues of Op. 20 with, say, the finales of Op. 9 and Op. 17, we can hear just how much more the quartet aims towards the final cadence of the last movement. Where the earlier quartets tail off gracefully, the fugue pushes hard to the very end. Arguably, it is from Haydn's Op. 20 that the gigantic fugal designs in Beethoven's late instrumental music, the finale of his "Hammerklavier" Sonata (1818) and especially his *Grosse Fuge* (1826, as the finale of the Quartet in B♭, Op. 130), derive their awe-inspiring power.

One might well ask: what is it about the earlier movements of three of the Op. 20 quartets that makes these fugal endings satisfying? Is something missing earlier on, which a dynamic fugue can supply, a shortcoming that has to be put right, or are there loose ends that the fugue is able to tie together? Or is it that a finale can add an extra dimension to the quartet as a whole, making it greater than the sum of its four movements, and that Haydn's fugues do this very well?

I am inclined to think that the latter is closer to the truth. Consider the example most consistently offered of a piece whose ending ties together the loose threads of earlier movements, the C major quartet from Op. 20. To my ears, its first three movements are no more in need of a fugal finale than are those of the E♭ quartet from the same set, for which Haydn composed a mercurial 160-bar Presto in 2/4 (about four minutes of music, including full repeats). Both quartets begin with moderately paced sonata movements of just over a hundred bars, and both have slow movements that are characterized by special textures and minuet move-

Table 3.3
(*cont.*)

68	73	76	83	92	99	129	151	156
continuation	statement	continuation	episode	exposition (2 entries)	episode	nonfugal section	statement	coda
	G			F		(C)	C	
	V			IV → V/IV		(I)	I	

ments whose trios are incomplete in form and tonality. Yet their finales are entirely different: No. 2 is a through-composed fugue that starts out quietly and
ends with a loud unison passage, whereas No. 1 is a sonata form with repeats,
using a variety of textures at various dynamic levels but ending quietly.[12]

What may be of more significance for the finales of Op. 20 is the novelty—for
Haydn—of fugal texture. That is, the fugue of No. 2, being a fugue, is a more
special type of movement for a string quartet of around 1770 than is the sonata
form of the Presto in Eb. The delicate textures and sprightly character of the
Presto recall the finales of Op. 17 nos.1, 5, and 6, and, to a lesser extent, Op. 17,
No. 2, and Op. 9, Nos. 2 and 5; they are pretty much what we expect a finale to
be.

And we should not forget that the genre of fugal finale was not Haydn's invention. At least one quartet by an older composer active in Mannheim, Frantisek
Xaver Richter, had appeared in print by 1768, and Haydn had undoubtedly
heard others by Johann Georg Albrechtsberger and other composers of his generation;[13] it is perhaps more surprising that Haydn did not write any fugues for
Op. 9 or for Op. 17 than that he included some in his next set. The fugal legacy of
Op. 20, in any event, showed Haydn's superiority in yet another medium, hence
a further justification for his being regarded as the leading composer of the day.

4

Quartet in F Minor, Op. 20, No. 5

The F minor quartet from Op. 20 has consistently held a place in the front rank of Haydn's so-called celebrated quartets. It is a work worth studying from many points of view. For the first violin, the Adagio is one of the great solos of the chamber music repertory. For the ensemble as a whole, the variety of textures in the other movements makes the work an ideal proving ground for chamber music playing. For the listener outside the quartet, there is much musical interest throughout; the coda to the opening Moderato, with its tightly controlled modulation to remote keys, is merely one of the high points.

MODERATO

The Moderato is in a sonata form that exhibits some freedom from the textbook norm. The basic division of the movement into exposition, development, recapitulation, and coda is straightforward, and there are distinct thematic ideas—first and second "subjects"—in the home key and the relative major. The material differences between the exposition and recapitulation are striking, however, with about a third of the recapitulation newly composed. For instance, in the exposition the opening theme, suitably transposed, initiates the second group; were the recapitulation to follow the course of the exposition, this theme would have to be played in F minor at both points, and the suppression of its second appearance is an obvious stratagem. Other changes will merit more detailed discussion.

The exposition begins with two statements of the main theme. The antecedent resolves onto the tonic in bar 5, making the downbeat of that bar a point of harmonic closure and phrase elision. The consequent, by contrast, reaches the dominant and is thus harmonically open-ended, but it appears to lose its direction once the appoggiatura chord in bar 12 resolves a bar later. Haydn had reached the same position in the first movement of the quartet in D minor, Op. 9, No. 4, and it is instructive to see him using the earlier quartet as a model for his escape from a thematic impasse (see Example 4.1): the third of the dominant chord is lowered, and the resulting minor dominant becomes chord III of the relative major, the key of the second group.

Example 4.1 (a) Op. 9, No. 4, i, bars 13–17

(b) Op. 20, No. 5, i, bars 11–15

In both pieces, it is the cello's repeated notes that carry the rhythm through the modulation. In the later quartet, Haydn aims the top line of the consequent phrase of the first subject at the appoggiatura f^1–$e\natural^1$ so that the modulation can flow seamlessly from the dominant. We can also understand why Haydn resolves the dissonance at bar 12 into a kind of slow trill: it enables the cello to pick up the rhythmic activity of the upper strings and so lead the music into the new key without a break. The complementary rhythms across bars 13–14—eighth notes in the upper parts with the cello at rest, followed by the upper parts at rest with eighth notes in the cello—enables the whole of the first group to proceed virtually without pause.

If the continuity of the first group justifies a brief rest before the start of the second (see Example 4.2), the manner of its execution is at first puzzling. The first violin db^2 in bar 18 is the end point of the arpeggio on the dominant seventh, but it cannot resolve because the next theme—the first subject, transposed to A♭ major—must begin on ab^1, not c^2. The "lead-in" inserted at bar 19 aims at ab^1, but sounds as if it were awkwardly tacked on to the new section as a way of bridging the fourth between db^2 and ab^1.

Example 4.2 Op. 20, No. 5, i, bars 17–20

It is sometimes said that these moments are a feature of Haydn's earlier style and that in works of a later date "transition figures and phrases are almost completely eliminated";[1] it would seem that this lead-in is an instance of such a transition figure. If the purpose of such a figure is to call attention to the break between the first and second groups and thus to highlight the uninterrupted progress up to this point but not beyond it, then the challenge facing Haydn would be to play out the consequences of this intrusion later in the movement. He cannot do so at the equivalent place in the recapitulation because the opening theme of the piece is suppressed at the start of the second group. Instead, the lead-in introduces the start of recapitulation (Example 4.3). This naturally dramatic moment in the form is intensified because the lead-in figure appears *earlier* than the listener expects it; and this intensity is enhanced by rhythmic modification of the initial figure (triplets instead of ordinary sixteenths) and by its threefold repetition. The sudden *pianissimo* also has consequences further along: Haydn's surprise *forte* at the repeat of the theme four bars later establishes an angry, aggressive mood for the consequent phrase and transition, which is utterly at odds with the parallel passage in the exposition.

The coda of this movement has rightly been seen as a high point in Haydn's art of harmony. Since it follows directly from the repeat of the development and recapitulation, it will be useful to trace its origins from the music around the repeat sign at bar 48. In the first and second endings for the exposition, Haydn returns to another procedure first used in Op. 9, No. 4, the enharmonic reinterpretation of the flattened sixth of the relative major: fb^2, a neighbor note in A♭, is

Example 4.3 Op. 20, No. 5, i, bars 82–5

respelled as e♮¹, the leading note of F minor, and so prepares the repeat of the exposition (Example 4.4a). In the second ending, the harmony moves to D♭ major and so f♭¹/e♮¹ disappears from the melody. The coda also starts in D♭, now approached from F minor. The earlier e♮ harmonic play in the melody is replaced by the opposition of e♮ and e♭ in the cello (Example 4.4b).

Example 4.4 Op. 20, No. 5, i, (a) bars 46–49

(b) Bars 134–136

But the start of the coda (Example 4.5) is based on the main second-group theme, which has a different starting note. This gives the g♭¹ first heard in bar 48a an important role in the partwriting, as neighbor to f¹. What happens in the coda is a reversal of this relationship: in bar 138 g♭¹ is still an upper neighbor; a bar later f¹ is a leading note to g♭¹. But by spelling out this reversal so clearly, Haydn prepares the way for a further surprise, a change of mode to the very remote G♭ *minor* in bar 142, whose mystery is underscored by the unusual dynamic marking *piano assai*. This new harmony is itself elaborated, by a progression to its own relative major (B♭♭) implied at the downbeat of bar 144. In the rest of this extraordinary passage, the harmony reverses through G♭ minor (bar 145) and D♭ (bar 146). After a passage of extraordinary intensity, Haydn unleashes a ferocious prolongation of the tonic $^6_4$ chord, followed by two I–IV–V–I cycles before the harmony collapses, exhausted, to a V–I *pianissimo*.[2]

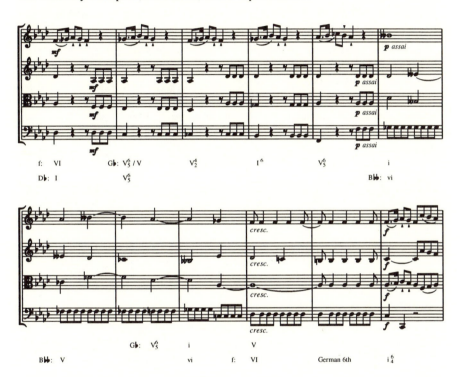

Example 4.5 Op. 20, No. 5, i, bars 137–148

As was noted in chapter 2 in the section on "ideal" quartet textures and themes, the opening violin solo develops its rhythmic shape from the accompaniment pattern, but this arrangement and its variants account for only a quarter of the first movement. There is a shift away from first-violin melodic domination, and extended returns of the opening texture are found only at the start of the development, recapitulation, and coda. In the first group, two bars of trio sonata (bars 10–11) lead to a section in which the three upper strings join forces against the cello (bars 12–16), from which a solo violin cadenza provides an escape. In the second group the texture becomes more stratified, with greater interest in the inner parts. The new second-group theme starts with the instruments paired, the high register of the viola increasing the tension between the opposing lines. In the much reduced restatement of this theme (Example 4.6) the inner parts resume their normal position, and the second violin remains stationary during the elaboration of the II$_5^6$ chord at *(a)*. The change of harmony two bars later, to a diminished seventh, is marked by a reduction of the half-bar motive to a single chord, *(b)*, and a further reduction to a single note, *(c)*. This f^2, which appears to leap out from the previous chord, marks the start of a new "voice" for the first violin: the e♭^{2} embellished by its lower neighbor, at *(d)*, behaves like a *messa di voce*, enabling the second violin to resolve the unanswered c♭^{2} in bar 35 and take over the principal motive, at *(e)*. When the first violin again becomes the highest moving part, the second violin takes over the e♭^{2}, at *(f)*, this time embellished by both upper and lower neighbors. In other words, as the first violin climbs ever higher from bar 32 onwards, the second violin is called upon to take its place both registrally and in the presentation of material.

Example 4.6 Op. 20, No. 5, i, bars 28–38

The textures in the development and recapitulation are, for the most part, taken from the exposition, though the insistent sixteenth notes in the second violin become increasingly prominent (compare bars 37–38 with bars 89–97, 125–26, and 131–32). Also of interest is a poignant phrase in the recapitulation, given in Example 4.7, which acts as a bridge between the first modulation (Example 4.1) and the more daring harmonies of the coda (Example 4.5). Its appearance radically alters the shape of the recapitulation, obliging Haydn to return to an earlier point: bars 123 marks the repetition of material from material in bars 113 and following. Texturally it is not quite the same as the passages it recalls and anticipates: the first violin continues to have a melodic role over slow-moving inner parts and the cello's eighth-note pulse.

Example 4.7 Op. 20, No. 5,i, bars 119–23

MENUET AND TRIO

The minuet, a sonata form in miniature, develops two ideas deriving from the first movement: the neighbor-note relation between D♭ and C, and repeated notes in the accompaniment. Of these, the neighbor note is easier to follow: its appearance in the bass across bars 3–4, as part of an augmented sixth chord and its resolution, immediately precedes a passage in which d♭ is reinterpreted as the seventh of the relative major. The second half starts out with another harmonization of c^2–d♭^{2}, V–I in the subdominant, B♭ minor. The augmented sixth is used again to prepare the return of F minor, but now the D♭–C is at the very bottom of the cello's range and the open C's are, characteristically, reinforced by the viola at the upper octave.

The piece is carried forward not so much by melodic development as by the rhythmic movement of its accompaniment. (In the first movement, the eighth-note accompaniment figure has a similar generative function.) The quarter-note pulse is immediately taken up by the first-violin melody, and the repeated note figure takes two forms: one starts with an octave leap at *(a)* and initiates a two-bar figure; the other preserves the threefold literal repetition at *(b)* and forms a response to the c^2–d♭^{2}–c^2 neighbor. Both of these are, in turn, further developed. From *(b)* we get a general quarter-note motion, as can be seen from the immediate continuation at *(c)* and the return of the repeated notes in the bass at *(d)*. From *(a)* are derived the more striking figures with larger leaps, at *(e)*, eventually leading to a suppression of the first beat, at *(f)*. This last version is particularly effective when set against the repeat of the opening or a continuation into the second half of the movement: a sudden *forte* is implicit in the former, and specified in the latter.

Example 4.8 Op. 20, No. 5, ii, bars 1–20

The Trio, set in the tonic major, is more relaxed, despite its preponderance of irregular phrases. It contains fewer changes of texture, and these seem more predictable: trio sonata leading to lightly accompanied violin solo. The repeated-note motive, first confined to the cello, is used as a tonic pedal for the violin's descent through the fourth f^1–e^1–d^1–c^1. As it continues down towards low a, the viola, which was silent for the first three bars, takes over the cello's quarter-note pulse and reverses the violin's fourth. The eighth notes of the violin solo are left unaccompanied, so that the repeated note figure is once again reduced to two quarter notes in bars 60, 62, and 63.

For the middle section (Example 4.9), a more dancelike texture is introduced, in the manner of a serenade. The first violin continues with the melody, but the dynamic marking remains *piano*, and so it must struggle to be heard above the cello's oompah bass (whose effect is accentuated by the open C) and the second violin's inner-voice doodling in imitation of a wind-band clarinet.

But if the overall design and style of the Trio seems straightforward—trio sonata over F major pedal, violin solo modulating to C major, serenade on the dominant leading back to the beginning —the recapitulation offers some surprises. The cadential figure in bars 92–93 loses a bar (compare bars 64–69 with bars 89–93) and thus seems to demand further music. This "coda" (Example 4.10), almost an afterthought in its effect, makes use of textures more characteristic of the quartet, with the lower instruments taking the moving parts until the violin returns for the final cadence.

Example 4.9 Op. 20, No. 5, ii, bars 70–77

Example 4.10 Op. 20, No. 5, ii, bars 94–99

ADAGIO

Haydn had already cast one of his slow movements in Op. 9 and one in Op. 17 as sicilianos. With only two exceptions, he was to use this type of dance in each subsequent set of six quartets. The broad melodic lines of this Adagio, with its frequent use of a dotted-note figure in the first half of the bar, is typical of the genre. So are its regular phrase structure and the alternation of quarter note and eighth note for the basic accompaniment pattern. Texture is dominated almost throughout by the first violin, much more than in the Adagio of Op. 9, No. 1 (discussed in chapter 2): passages of melodic interest for the second violin merely allow the first to behave even more like a soloist, with faster runs in an improvised style. Contrast is provided only in two places, bars 28–35 and bars 72–79 (Haydn's *tenuto* marking in bar 28 is addressed to the viola but applies to all four instruments), a closing theme that suggests more interdependence.

The decorative quality of the Adagio is well suited to theme-and-variations treatment, and the first sixteen bars suggest this form. (In later quartets, the siciliano is a popular candidate for variation movements.) But the overall design of the movement is a sonata, and this is neatly articulated by the contrasting rhythmic patterns in the two main themes (Example 4.11): for the closing subject, in the dominant, the dotted figure appears in the second half of the bar, reversing the normal siciliano pattern that governs the opening theme.

Example 4.11 Op. 20, No. 5, iii, (a) bars 1–2, first violin

(b) Bars 28–31, first violin

Though the dramatic qualities of sonata form are underplayed, a four-bar phrase at the end of the development stands out for its unusual harmonic bearing. This passage, which has elicited much commentary in the literature, is special on account of two notations, unique in Haydn's output of quartets: the continuo figuring of the cello part, and the remark *per figuram retardationis* in the solo violin.

The meaning of the bass figures is clear: they are not instructions to a keyboard player, but rather clarify that the basic harmony is determined by the three lower string parts. The remark *per figuram retardationis*, on the other hand, has no antecedent in the eighteenth century: the term *retardatio* was sometimes used for a suspension that resolves upwards by step instead of downwards, but that meaning cannot apply here. The normal interpretation is that the solo violin is playing behind the harmony and thus attempts to slow down the harmonic pacing of the accompaniment. There is already a precedent in this Adagio for rhythmic disagreement between the parts: the hemiola in bar 26 puts the solo violin out of synchronism with the accompaniment, and the triplet figures in bars 19 and 23 also have a metrically unsettling effect. The harmonic rhythm of the violin part is never in doubt in the exposition, but in the *figura retardationis* the unbroken run of thirty-second notes, rife with appoggiaturas, makes a separate set of chord changes difficult. At any rate, the first violin does not lag behind the rest of the ensemble by a fixed amount of time, or even by an integral number of eighth-note beats.

A clue may, however, be provided by the fact that Haydn's remark is not aligned with the beginning of the passage, but is written over the last group of thirty-second notes in bar 53. This suggests that the solo violin is correctly positioned for most of the first bar of the passage, embellishing the chords that support it by making the first note of each group of thirty-seconds a member of the underlying chord: d^2–f^2–a^2 in the first half of the bar, d^2–$f\sharp^2$–c^3 in the second. The embellishment of each chord is initiated by a short ornament: the double neighbor-note d^2–$c\sharp^2$–e^2–d^2 (–f^2) at *(a)*, and the turn figure d^2–$c\sharp^2$–d^2–e^2 (–$f\sharp^2$) at *(b)*. We find recurrences or transpositions of these initial patterns for each of the subsequent harmonies, as is shown in Example 4.12, the solo violin lagging behind the underlying harmony by about two eighth-note beats from bar 54. Diagonal lines show the "correct" harmonic alignment; dotted slurs show recurrences of the initial embellishing figures for *(a)* and *(b)*, and solid slurs show the elaboration of the underlying chords.

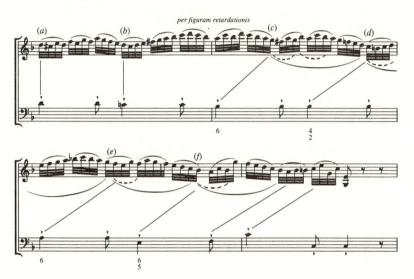

Example 4.12 Op. 20, No. 5, iii, bars 53–56, first violin and cello, with Haydn's bass figures

From this analysis, some patterns emerge: *(c)* follows *(a)* in its use of two double neighbor figures, *(d)* follows *(b)* with its lower neighbor plus an ascending octave scale, while *(e)* and *(f)* both use a double neighbor plus a descending scale in strict sequence. Of course, the rhythmic displacement helps to conceal these relationships, because it is working on two levels: the basic delaying by two eighth-note beats, and the finely tuned adjustments at the thirty-second-note level. But the analysis shows that Haydn's art of displacement has been carefully thought out.[3]

The subsequent history of the eighteenth-century quartet siciliano shows Haydn's unease with a style that risks domination by the first violin as virtuoso soloist. In Op. 33 he made it the finale of the G major quartet, and used the variation form to distribute interest to the other parts. This movement inspired a more elaborate set of variations, the finale of Mozart's quartet in D Minor, K. 421, in which the potential of the lower instruments as soloists is more fully realized.[4] The Adagio of Haydn's Op. 50, No. 1, is also cast in this form, and solos for other instruments are again distributed across the variations. In the quartets of the 1790s, the siciliano movements become more stylized. In the Adagio of Op. 71, No. 1, the distinction between melody and accompaniment in the outer sections is undermined, as all four instruments participate in the characteristic dance rhythms. In Op. 76, No. 2, the violin once again assumes its role as soloist, but without the consistency of accompaniment to which it is accustomed: *pizzicato* strumming and *legato*, *portato*, and *staccato* bow strokes alternate unpredictably to create an overall impression of a free accompaniment working within the framework of a strict ternary form with coda.

The fugal finale is discussed in chapter 3.

5

Quartet in A Major, Op. 20, No. 6

Until we reach the fugal finale, the A major quartet has close connections with Haydn's earlier quartets. The bright key and lively 6/8 tempo mark the opening Allegro di molto e scherzando as a "fiddle piece," closely related to Op. 9, No. 6, and Op. 17, No. 6, and stylistically derived from the opening 3/8 and 6/8 Presto movements from Op. 1 and Op. 2. The Adagio is, in effect, an aria for violin of the sort encountered throughout the first twenty-two quartets; the "varied reprise" of its exposition links it more specifically to a few slow movements in Op. 9 and Op. 17. In the minuet, the reduced scoring of the trio section recalls the three-part texture of an earlier trio, Op. 9, No. 4, and a general tendency to spell out the contrast between the minuet and the trio.

ALLEGRO DI MOLTO E SCHERZANDO

To call a quartet movement a fiddle piece may seem tautologous, since all Classical quartet movements, with the exception of some fugues, are musically led by the first violin part. What I mean by the term is that features of violin virtuosity come to the fore. A major is a bright key because it favors the upper register of the instruments by emphasizing the higher open strings: E as the dominant, A as the tonic, and D as the subdominant; even when the open strings are not actually used, they resonate sympathetically with stopped notes at the same or related pitches. The 6/8 meter encourages simple dancelike accompaniments, of which the pattern of comprising an eighth rest and two eighth notes is the most characteristic. The liveliness of Haydn's tempo marking is accentuated by the purpose to which he puts his fastest note values, apart from ornaments: simple scales and broken chords, and two-note snap figures.

The tessitura of the quartet is also high, and not just because the first violin is always active on the upper strings: the cello rarely needs its C string, and there are extended passages in which it is playing about an octave above its normal register within the staff lines of the bass clef. The very opening gives us some idea of this textural compression: the octave separating the first violin and the cello at the beginning soon proves inadequate to accommodate the inner parts. Elsewhere, the viola behaves like a third violin, for instance in the final minor-key passage in the second group (Example 5.1); it continues in a high register in the closing theme (see Example 5.5b, later in this chapter).

Example 5.1 Op. 20, No. 6, i, bars 45–50

Insofar as the material in the exposition is recapitulated in the tonic in its original order, the form of this sonata movement is straightforward. In between the development section starts with new material and becomes harmonically discursive; it then settles in the relative minor and ends with a recall of the closing theme.

Despite the regular shape of the exposition, there is an uneasy progression from the first group to the second. To begin with, the opening idea is more a self-contained two-bar motto than a well-formed theme, and leads initially to a weak cadence in bar 4, with the third of the tonic in the upper part. The counterstatement that follows lasts longer but still finishes weakly. Yet another statement of the theme follows, in bar 11 (see Example 5.2). The change of dynamics to *piano* makes it sound like a concluding gesture, both as an echo of the very opening and as a completion of the A major business in bars 7–10. But it also marks the start of the first motivic development in the piece, which will soon lead to the dominant.

The E major reached at bar 22 (Example 5.3a) sounds tentative, partly because it comes in the middle of a phrase, and partly because it is scored for violin duet. The long slur across bars 19–24, which instructs the first violin to play on the G string, further prevents the full force of an arrival in a new key from being unleashed; that must await the conclusion of the phrase (Example 5.3b) in which Haydn masterfully shows his sensitivity to violin tone color.

Example 5.2 Op. 20, No. 6, i, bars 9–15

Example 5.3 Op. 20, No. 6, i, (a) bars 22–23

(b) Bars 28–30

The caesura in bar 38 sets up the next theme as the main idea of the second group, and it is indeed the longest. But it starts off in E minor and proves harmonically unstable; even after spending fourteen bars reestablishing the key, it continues to tread warily between minor and major before cadencing definitively in major eleven bars later .

This theme at bar 31 was a favorite of Donald Tovey's, and Tovey never tired of comparing it to a similarly positioned E minor theme in the opening Allegro vivace from Beethoven's Sonata Op. 2, No. 2.[1] He attributed to Beethoven a "new technique of development," necessary to accommodate both Mozart's regularity and Haydn's freedom of form. In the Beethoven sonata, tension is increased by the inexorable stepwise ascent of the bass, which is contrasted with the "improvisation and ruminating" by which Haydn will "drift towards E major."[2] To be fair, the two themes are so different in character—one is lyrical, the other developmental—that comparing them is of limited use. It is possible, however, that Beethoven had Haydn's theme in mind when he came to write another work, the quartet Op. 18, No. 5, one which moreover starts with an A major Allegro in 6/8. Beethoven's transitional theme (Example 5.4) is, if anything, more relaxed than Haydn's, and makes its way to the harmonic goal by the direct juxtaposition of E minor and major a few bars later. Haydn, by contrast, uses the more Beethovenian sequential technique (as Tovey would describe it) to pull his harmony from the remote D major towards the goal of E major.

Example 5.4 Beethoven, Quartet in A, Op. 18, No. 5, i, bars 25–32

The closing theme of Haydn's Allegro di molto, the only one in the movement that is metrically regular (2 plus 2 bars), merits special attention. It unmistakably recalls the closing theme from Op. 9, No. 6, having the identical phrase structure and giving prominence to C♯ minor through the emphasis of G♯ major as a secondary dominant (Example 5.5). Its unstable metric position, though, forces a phrase elision on the downbeat of bar 61, with the effect that the whole of the passage from bars 31 to the end of the exposition is an unbroken unit, in sharp contrast to the fitful first group and modulation.

Example 5.5 Op. 9, No. 6, i, (a) bars 42–45

(b) Op. 20, No. 6, i, bars 55–59

The development begins elusively with new material, and settles in F♯ minor with an extended virtuoso display based on figuration presented earlier. A variation on the closing theme, this time starting on the downbeat, is used to return to the home key (Example 5.6); an additional bar's rest increases the excitement with which the principal motive is anticipated.[3]

Not only are the themes of the movement recapitulated in order, there is relatively little recomposition within or between them: of the 64 bars in the exposition, the first 4 and last 46 reappear in the recapitulation in their original and suitably transposed forms, respectively. The new material, which replaces the counterstatements of the main theme and the modulation to the dominant, adds to the play between minor and major in the second group.

Example 5.6 Op. 20, No. 6/i bars 103–9

ADAGIO

The Adagio is a type of sonata movement with varied repeats, a form devised by Carl Philipp Emanuel Bach around 1760 and cultivated by him during the following decade. In the binary movements of Bach's *Sonaten mit veränderten Reprisen*, each half is written out twice, with embellishments added the second time, rather than marked with repeat signs. Haydn used Bach's design principle for five quartet slow movements written between 1769 and 1781, each time with one important modification to the original idea: the second half of each movement is heard only once, so that the overall shape of the movement is a_1–a_2–b. The 27-bar a_1-section in Op. 20, No. 6, is the exposition of a sonata form, with a move to the dominant at bar 15 and a new idea in B major, albeit one that is rhythmically related to the opening theme. The embellishments in a_2 include more fast runs and arpeggios; the counterstatements of the opening theme in a_1 and a_2, compared in Example 5.7, exemplify Haydn's idea of the varied reprise. The operatic-heroic character of the solo violin is, naturally, accentuated by these embellishments, which sometimes result in additional leaps between registers, as at the end of bar 40.

Example 5.7 Op. 20, No. 6, ii, (a) bars 9–14, first violin

(b) Bars 36–41, first violin

The b-section functions as a reprise on two levels. It reverses the harmonic direction of the exposition by starting with the first theme in the dominant, moving further afield (in the manner of a development section) for several bars before returning to the home key in time for a recapitulation of the second theme. More interesting is the curtailment of the rhythmic activity in the first violin, with nothing shorter than a sixteenth note. This makes for an overall ternary shape for the solo part, with virtuoso ornamentation only in the second of its three formal units. Nonetheless, the vocal quality of the first violin is preserved throughout, and is actually enhanced by the numerous sustained notes—some as long as a bar and a half—in the b–section. Note, for instance, how the long $g\natural^2$ (functioning as $f\text{x}^2$) in bar 57, pointing towards the key of C$\sharp$ minor, is recalled in the unexpected shift to E minor at bar 73, only a few bars before the final cadence (Example 5.8).

Example 5.8 Op. 20, No. 6, ii, (a) bars 57–58, first violin and cello

(b) Bars 72–75, first violin and cello

Yet there are also features of the movement that point to Haydn's originality in both form and texture. To begin with, he has modified Bach's sonata plan in a number of ways. At the lowest level, a lightly embellished dominant seventh chord in the first a-section (bar 20) turns into a miniature cadenza in the varied reprise (bar 44) and thus briefly halts the metric flow towards the cadence on the dominant.

At the highest level, of course, the reprise of the b-section is absent. This is characteristic of Haydn's appropriation of Bach (all four quartet slow movements in question include a varied reprise only of the a-section) as it allows him to show his skills at both development of a form and embellishment of a melody without creating a movement of disproportionate length. In this Adagio, the b-section is about the same length of each a-section and returns to the simpler melodic style of the a_1.

Perhaps the most interesting modification, though, is to be found in the foreshortening of the second a-section. After its cadential trill, a_1 ended with a three-bar codetta that gently rounded off the section by bringing the melodic line into a lower octave (Example 5.9a). The varied reprise, however, omits the codetta, the resolution of its trill being elided to the start of the b-section by the action of a grace note (Example 5.9b). The b-section duly ends with a transposed, lightly varied repeat of the original codetta (Example 5.9c), whose rounding-off function is underscored by the *pianissimo* in the penultimate bar, the composer's only dynamic marking in the movement. Here is yet another excellent example of Haydn's freedom of form, in which an essentially binary design is modified by a pattern of endings that suggests a ternary design while at the same time propelling the music across the boundary between the two binary halves.[4]

Example 5.9 Op. 20, No. 6, ii, (a) bars 24–27

(b) Bars 51–53

(c) Bars 76–79

If the Adagio harks back to the quartets of the previous decade, with the first violin leading as prima donna, there are nevertheless some innovations in the part-writing. The second violin's characteristic sixteenth-note groups (see

Example 5.10a) appear to be a simple embellishment, one that gently animates the rhythm. Where the music reaches the dominant, however, the three-note figure is extended to a longer flourish, which assumes principal melodic interest as the first violin engages the viola in a duet (Example 5.10b). This procedure, whereby increased interest in one inner part stimulates new relationships for the first violin, culminates in the b–section, where the cello is finally persuaded to give up its role of providing the pulse to make up a trio of counterpoint against the second violin (Example 5.10c). Although the integration of theme and accompaniment can hardly be said to be a primary feature of this Adagio, this last passage may nevertheless be understood as the result of a gradual involvement of the inner parts in thematic material, a process that had begun as early as the ninth bar of the movement.

Example 5.10 Op. 20, No. 6, ii, (a) bar 9

(b) Bars 15–16

(c) Bars 65–67

MENUET

The opening theme of this movement bears close resemblance to the start of the Allegro di molto e scherzando; this may explain why Haydn takes the unprecedented step of putting an interior slow movement before the minuet in a four-movement string quartet. The brevity and aphoristic quality of the main section is enhanced by the informal retrograde at the first double bar (compare bar 7 with bars 9–10) and by the quotation of the opening four bars at the end, where one also finds the movement's only dynamic marking, *pianissimo*.

The Trio is for three instruments, all of which are, unusually, marked *sopra una corda*. All the parts sound in their lowest register, in this respect anticipating the Scherzo of the C major quartet from Op. 33. But whereas the movement from the later work relies on registral contrast for its effect (the trio is a birdlike duet for the violins), here Haydn uses the darker tone color to help maintain a quiet dynamic, and also to join the low-register ending of the Minuet, on c$\sharp^1$, to its middle-register beginning, on a^1. A further connection between minuet and trio may be seen in the cello's connective A major arpeggio as a thematic link with the Trio (see the brackets in Example 5.11).

Example 5.11 Op. 20, No. 6, iii, bars 15–24

The fugal finale is discussed in chapter 3.

6

Quartet in C Major, Op. 20, No. 2

The C major quartet from Op. 20 is one of the supreme achievements of the Classical period, and its traditional omission from the category of Haydn's "celebrated" quartets—which for years amounted to exclusion from the canon—must be reckoned as one of the great puzzles of chamber music reception. Throughout the work, one can see the composer's invention in full flow: a first movement whose main theme is polyphonic, led by the cello from above; a slow movement of great rhetorical power in a thoroughly unconventional design; a minuet that recapitulates ideas from earlier movements; and a finale that, though cast as a fugue, questions its fugality soon after the exposition and appears to renounce it altogether well before the ending. The quartet is a marvellous repository of textures, and these will merit closer study in context.

MODERATO

On the face of it, this sonata form movement seems oddly proportioned: its recapitulation is only twenty-six bars long, barely half the length of the forty-seven-bar exposition. The proportions between these sections, though extreme, are nevertheless consistent with Haydn's early sonata forms. In all but one of the opening sonata movements from Op. 9 and Op. 17, the recapitulation is shorter; in two cases, it is only three-fifths the length of the exposition.

As always, it helps to look at the specific procedures to understand the movement's asymmetry. What sets this Moderato apart is its elaborate contrapuntal opening. Almost parodying the eighteenth-century trio sonata, Haydn begins the quartet with two upper voices—cello and second violin—above the viola as bass. The texture cannot be mistaken for fugue, since Haydn would have started a fugue with two contrapuntal lines rather than three, but it is fugal practice that determines the restatements of the opening theme, and thus the shape of the first group, shown in Table 6.1.

Table 6.1

The "fugal" organization of the first group of the Moderato of Op. 20, No. 2

Bar	1–6	7–14	15–21
Material	theme + link	theme + continuation	theme + continuation
Tonality and function	C: I → V/V	G: I	C: I–V^7/IV–IV–I–II^6–V

This arrangement is, of course, very different from the usual procedure of beginning with a harmonically open antecedent thematic phrase, which ends on the dominant and needs to be answered by a consequent, or by a complete statement of a theme in the tonic followed by a counterstatement. Here, the first group comprises three statements of the opening trio sonata texture, in the tonic, the dominant, and again in the tonic. The first two are joined together by a modulatory link bar, which owes nothing to fugal technique though it neatly anticipates the first violin's tonal answer by outlining an ascending fifth from c^1 to g^1 (see the square brackets in Example 6.1a). The second statement leads to a full close in G major (Example 6.1b) with more quartet-like animation in the inner parts; the accompanying *messa di voce* bursts into a trill and is thus more self-consciously vocal than a simple held note.

Example 6.1 Op. 20, No. 2, i, (a) bars 5–7

(b) Bars 11–13

(b) (*cont.*) bars 14–16

The unusual beginning affects the course of the movement. Because there is so much G major in the first group, a formal modulation in the exposition would be anticlimactic, and so the dominant in bar 21 leads immediately to the start of the second group in G major. And since a modulation to the dominant is in any event out of place in the recapitulation, Haydn discards the fugal plan entirely, collapsing the first group into the space of less than five bars.

As one can infer from Example 6.2, the start of the second group is also omitted in the recapitulation. The reason for this may be that there is a prominent appoggiatura on the dominant that prepares the recapitulation (bar 80), and one also midway through the principal second group theme (bar 85). The start of the second group was prepared in a similar way in the exposition, and its recapitulation here would have led to three identical appoggiatura figures in close succession.

Example 6.2 Op. 20, No. 2, i, bars 80–85·

The distribution of parts in the opening—the cello has the melody in a high register—has often been noted as a special feature of Op. 20, No. 2, almost the defining characteristic of the first movement. Cello melodies were, however, common enough in the quartets of Haydn's contemporaries, and one cannot describe the opening of the Moderato as novel in this respect. The top voice could, of course, have been taken by the viola, but Haydn's arrangement may have been determined by observing that the viola is more effective as a mid-register bass part that can exploit the resonance of its open C string (Example 6.3).

Example 6.3 Op. 20, No. 2, i, bars 1–(6), viola

Normal fugal technique would require the parts to be swapped around in restatements of the subject. But when the first violin takes the theme in bar 7, the viola and second violin repeat their parts in the dominant at bar 7 rather than moving on to different strands of the polyphony. Why is this so? If the appropriate response to an opening cello solo is an entry from the normal leading instrument, the first violin, then the main theme must be heard not a fifth higher, but an octave and a fifth higher, that is the first violin must also play near the top of its range to answer the cello effectively. The second violin could, of course, have taken over the bass line from the viola, but that would have left the viola supporting the violin in an uncomfortably high register. So Haydn sacrifices the customary redistribution of fugal parts so that the viola part can remain idiomatic. The open G string, though not specified in bars 7–11, is nevertheless implied by the character of the part.

A detail in bar 15 corroborates Haydn's interest in the sonority of string instruments. The first violin has a brief snatch of the bass line (see Example 6.1b, above), but Haydn lowers the last note of the bar by an octave, to g. This small adjustment cannot be attributed merely to the natural fall of an octave just before a cadence, for the same octave leap is not used in any of the other places where it would have been available: in the viola in bar 7, the second violin in bar 61, and the cello in bar 63. But the low g is an open string, and so enables the first violin to contribute to the bass in a way that is commensurate to the viola in bars 1–14. Finally the cello reaches down to its bottom C in the next bar, at which point the contrapuntal texture is abruptly cut off.

If the opening of the movement confers the impression that all four instruments have important roles in the first group, the type of part-writing that controls much of the second group, discussed briefly in chapter 2 in the discussion of "ideal" quartet textures, aims even more at equality in the part-writing. No fewer than three themes—beginning in bars 21, 30, and 33—set the two violins against the viola and cello with antiphonal duets in parallel thirds. (In the recapitulation, Haydn varies this by forming new pairs: first violin with cello in bar 89, first violin with viola in bar 92.) Between these themes he may favor the first violin with the melodic line (bars 23–24) or a brief virtuoso role (bars 31–32), or he may set the cello in a low register against the other strings (bars 28–29), but these changes are always part of an ongoing development of the paired-voice textures, and are not introduced merely for the sake of deliberate contrast.

The closing theme (see Example 6.4) illustrates Haydn's sensitivity to texture in a passage of great harmonic subtlety. It starts with the violins against the lower strings, the cello initially a tenth (not a third) below the viola at *(a)* so that it has enough space to make three octave leaps to reach high g^1, at *(b)*. The first violin, which has also reached its highest register, now becomes a soloist, with arpeggios reaching and descending from c^3, at *(c)*, its appoggiatura $e\flat^2$–d^2 implying a move to the minor. After the four-part chord in bar 38 duly resolves to a G minor triad, the cello wiggles out of its unison with the viola, at *(d)*, towards $e\flat^1$. The first violin follows with an imitation of the viola, at *(e)*, and then with variation, at *(f)*. Now it is the turn of the inner parts to animate the E$\flat$ chord, at *(g)*. The full cadence in G major at *(h)* initiates a four-bar codetta in *galant* style.

The part-writing at the start of the development section is much less idiomatic, and less integrated, with the second violin struggling wildly with broken chords against the exchanges between the first violin and cello. Haydn sometimes begins the development section with a texture that is unnatural to the quartet; this passage recalls the start of the development in Op. 9, No. 1, discussed in chapter 2 (see Example 2.1). The textural stratification in these thirteen bars highlights the unstable harmony and provides a foil for the rest of the development, where more sophisticated textures are developed to their fullest extent (Example 6.5). The polyphonic opening theme is presented in *stretto*, with the viola finally being assigned the theme and the cello the bass. A brief passage of paired strings leads to a return of the embellished slow chord progression from the second group. The outer parts again initiate the development, but the inner parts are given more scope to anchor the voice exchange between D$\sharp$ and F$\sharp$.

The dissonant second-violin d^2 in bar 70 is a remarkable detail. The voice exchange, together with the literal repetition in the inner parts in bars 68 and 69, sets up the expectation of a further repetition in bar 70. Instead, Haydn embellishes the c^2 with both the lower neighbor, the b^1 already heard, and the upper neighbor, d^2, which is new. This d^2 is expressive in its own right because it collides with the bass $d\sharp^1$ and is, moreover, a dissonance approached by leap. But it also can be heard as extending the neighbor figure c^2–b^1 by an extra note, d^2–c^2–b^1 across bars 69–70; this line is immediately stretched to a fourth, e^2–d^2–c^2–b^1.

Example 6.4 Op. 20, No. 2, i, bars 33–47

With the viola doubling a third below throughout, the way has been prepared for the closing subject to enter, a subtle reversal of material from the exposition (see the earlier Example 6.4).[1]

A final word about the form of the Moderato. All the "cuts" in the recapitulation just described can be justified musically, and what remains is still substantial enough to form the end of the second half of a binary form. Nevertheless, the movement has lost its sense of leisure: the early ambles through tonic and dominant in the fugal first group and the multiplicity of themes in the second are eliminated. That leisure, defined by the presence of more themes (or statements of themes) than are strictly necessary for formal clarity, is restored in the very strange movement that follows.

Example 6.5 Op. 20, No. 2, i, bars 61–73

CAPRICCIO: ADAGIO

The subtitle of this movement merits a brief explanation. It does not, of course, mean that the work is lighthearted in character, nor does Haydn use it in an ironical sense. Rather, the form of the movement is "free" in the sense understood by seventeenth- and eighteenth-century writers: instead of conforming to a recognizable movement plan, it makes its own way to new themes and keys; in modern parlance, it would be called a fantasia. Of course, it is usually preferable to think of well-composed music creating its own lines of development rather than following a preconceived plan;[2] and Haydn rarely gives the impression of being straitjacketed by fixed forms. Still, he recognizes here the special freedom of this Adagio, and will do so again a quarter of a century later when describing the slow movement of one of his last quartets.[3]

The Capriccio begins with a theme of great emotional intensity in C minor, with strongly dotted rhythms played loudly in unison and ending on the dominant. The consequent phrase is a restatement of the theme by the cello, accompanied quietly from above with chords in repeated sixteenth notes, their expressiveness enhanced by the *portato* markings. The theme now breaks into dotted rhythms that lead seamlessly to a long, freely developed violin solo, which from time to time alludes to the dotted rhythms but is mainly a fantasy on scales and broken chords, at times lightly accompanied. A modulation to the dominant brings a repeat of the cello version of the theme, in G minor; this too, leads via dotted rhythms back to the solo violin, but a half cadence in C minor is soon reached. Example 6.6 shows the end of the cello's theme in G minor, the dotted rhythms in all the parts, the emergent violin solo, and the half cadence. Taken on their own, the last four bars of Example 6.6 could well suggest that the movement may have come to an end and that we are about to hear a minuet in C major. But the proportions of what has come before argue against such an interpretation, as the long violin fantasy (bars 9–25) far outweighs what precedes or follows it.

Example 6.6 Op. 20, No. 2, ii, bars 28–33

Looking out over the abyss of the half cadence in bar 33, Haydn rescues the Capriccio by introducing a new, lyrical theme in E♭ major for the first violin, with serenade-like accompaniment. Although this theme offers a graceful "Classical" response to the aggressive, "Baroque" opening, the idea that it might function as a contrasting second subject soon proves illusory: a modulation leads from E♭ to its own dominant and the start of a new theme in that key in bar 42. There now follows a closing theme, at bar 46; the triplet sixteenth notes, with which this theme ends, have already been used extensively in the fantasy section, but no earlier material is actually quoted.

In other words, what might at first have appeared to be a second subject of a piece in C minor turns out to have been the first subject of an interpolation in E♭: a piece within a piece, so to speak. All this is learned after the fact, of course; but it is not difficult for the listener to remember collectively the broad events that have taken place and to understand the first fifty bars of the Capriccio as a conflation of two movement plans: one based on a ritornello, the other on sonata form (see Table 6.2).

Table 6.2
Formal plan of the Capriccio from Op. 20, No. 2

1–4	introduction	"Baroque" theme in C minor, played in unison
5–32	start of ritornello form	"Baroque" theme in C minor, as cello solo (5–8) free fantasy, led by first violin (9–25) "Baroque" theme in G minor, as cello solo (26–29) rounding-off on the dominant of C (30–33)
34–50	sonata form exposition	"Classical" theme in E♭ (34–37) modulation to dominant (38–41) second subject in B♭ (42–45) closing group, cadenza, final cadence (46–50)

What follows sounds like a development section, but it relates not just to the sonata exposition just heard but to the whole of the movement. The thoroughly conventional move to F minor (the supertonic of E♭) is achieved by a modified recall of part of the fantasy section, as can be seen by comparing the two extracts in Example 6.7; the continuation, however, is a transposition of the Classical theme to F minor.

A sequential, varied repetition of these opposing materials leads back to E♭, making bars 55–57 delicately poised between being a reprise of bar 34 and forming part of the ongoing developmental process. The triplets, which persist from bar 52 to the end of the movement, provide further integration of the two parts of the movement, since they figure prominently in both the fantasy section and the

Example 6.7 Op. 20, No. 2, ii, (a) bar 18

(b) Bars 51–54

accompaniment to the Classical theme. An ascending sequence lifts the music from E♭ through F minor to G major, the dominant of the original home key.

Example 6.8 Op. 20, No. 2, ii, (a) bar 33

Segue subito il Menuet

(b) Bars 61–63

A formal recapitulation is as unnecessary as it would be unwelcome. The first fifty bars had revealed a hybrid form, comprising elements of ritornello and a sonata slow movement. The last fourteen bars synthesize the two as a development section for the sonata, in E♭, and a preparation for a return of C minor. The Baroque theme was originally presented as an introductory gesture; a return to that introduction must be ruled out, since a recapitulation cannot begin with an introduction. And since the half cadence has already been diverted, at bar 34, to E♭, a return to that key or any other surprise harmony would equally be out of place. Despite the inconclusiveness of G major in bar 63, the only possible outcome is the start of a new movement.[4]

MENUET: ALLEGRETTO

The minuet and trio play out the opposition between the first two movements of the work, that is, the modest C major Moderato and the aggressive Baroque elements of the C minor Capriccio. The origins of the trio are easier to pin down. Its main theme is based on bars 6–7 of the Capriccio, turning a highly declamatory idea into a sequential pattern (Example 6.9); both the evening out of the rhythms and the appropriation of the inverted scoring—cello tune accompanied chordally from above—are also characteristic of trios.

Example 6.9 Op. 20, No. 2, (a) ii, bars 6–7

Trio

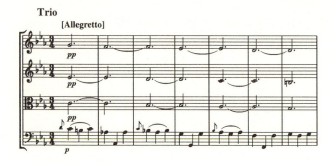

(b) iii, bars 57–63

The unison passage after the double bar recalls the rhetorical quality of fantasia elements in the Capriccio (see especially bars 51, 54, 57, and 59) and leads directly—without repeat—to a reprise of the minuet. The connection between the ends of the two movements is all the more remarkable for being less obvious (compare Example 6.8b with Example 6.10): in addition to recomposing the inner parts, Haydn also recalls the descent from the high g^2 to the lower octave.

Menuet da Capo

Example 6.10 Op. 20, No. 2, iii, bars 77–86

The relationship between the minuet and the opening Moderato is, as has been suggested, "intangible";[5] it is more a consequence of our hearing them as antipodes to the Capriccio and Trio than of shared material. The minuet is a small sonata-form movement, but unlike the Moderato it is cast much more as a solo piece: the first violin soars to b^3 just before the double bar and reaches c^4 in the recapitulation. (These are the highest notes in the entire Op. 20 set.) There is little sharing of motivic ideas, and only the vaguest of hints—in the violin parts only—of the duet textures that are so characteristic of the opening movement.

Moreover, the minuet is built up of irregular phrases, the first violin giving the impression almost of improvising its solo line. Bar 6 is weak on arrival, but becomes metrically strong as a result of the following four bars; much the same thing happens at bar 11, and in the reprise at bars 34 and 43. Against this irregular phrase organization, two eight-bar groups stand out: the central transition and the coda. In both, special techniques ensure that the first violin continues to dominate: double-stops in the transition, and *sopra una corda* in the coda. Indeed, both relate back to the opening violin solo, where a pedal g^1 is harnessed to the main theme. The extra resonance generated from within (the second violin doubles this pedal) is far more appropriate for a movement that stays within the range of *piano* to *pianissimo* than the more obvious technique of low-register open strings.

The interplay of register, both within the first violin part and across the entire texture, deserves special mention. Viewed on its own, the first violin part alternates between its lower and middle registers (in its opening phrase, the transition and the coda) and the high positions on the E string (in the "second group"). While the initial e^2 resolves to the proximate c^2 in bars 47–48, the melodic line of the minuet makes an overall descent to a lower register. (Double-stopping being impossible in the final phrase, the first violin's initial g^1 is converted into a second violin open-string pedal.)

This downward drift helps us also to understand the relationship of the trio to the main section of the minuet. Besides the contrasts already noted (cello taking over from first violin, C minor replacing C major), there is a crucial point of contact between the end of the coda and the beginning of the trio: the concluding c^1 in the first violin is transferred to the cello, a connection that Haydn strengthens by means of a thematic link, shown by brackets in Example 6.11.

Example 6.11 Op. 20, No. 2, iii, bars 53–58

The chordal accompaniment at the start of the trio is, of course, higher than the cello part, and this sets up a secondary level of registral interplay between the two sections of the movement. That is, the first violin's g^1 at the beginning of the trio can be heard as an afterimage of the pedal point accompanying the start of the minuet, to which it returns in the trio (bars 81ff.) to prepare the da capo. But the theme of the minuet, which occupies the space of the fourth between d^2 and g^2, is prepared by an earlier pedal in the trio, the first-violin g^2 at bars 77–80.

This is the highest note in the trio and, in conjunction with the second violin f#^{1}–g^1, distinctly recalls the transition phrase in the minuet (Example 6.12), with the pedal point and neighbor-note figure exchanged above the regular beating of the cello on G.

Example 6.12 Op. 20, No. 2, iii, (a) bars 21–24

(b) Bars 77–78

The fugal finale is discussed in chapter 3.

7

Quartet in G Minor, Op. 20, No. 3

This quartet is among the more enigmatic pieces in the repertory. It can scarcely be called a favorite among players or concert audiences, yet its relatively low public and private standing in no way bespeaks a lack of interest or originality. Indeed, the work is in so many respects unusual that it seems in places to defy interpretation. Many have commented on and occasionally described some of its problems, for example, the irregular phrase structure and the haunting interpolations in the Allegro con spirito;[1] but the quartet continues to prove resistant to analysis.

The broad picture is clear enough. The three G minor movements are similar in mood and also share thematic ideas; that much is characteristic of Classical works composed in minor keys. The outer movements are in sonata form, as is the main part of the Menuet. The Poco adagio might earn a textbook label of "rounded binary"; all that denies it sonata form status is Haydn's decision not to recapitulate the main theme in the tonic but to allow it instead to dominate a long development. The problems of form and tonality in the trio section of the Menuet will be addressed below.

ALLEGRO CON SPIRITO

Though the outlines of sonata form are clear enough in this movement, three features stand out as unusual: the proportions of the exposition, the interpolation of gestures that interrupt thematic development, and the tonal relationship of the start of the development to the start of the exposition. No theory is prescriptive on any of these matters, and Haydn's compositional freedom seems often defiantly at odds with what textbooks have to say about sonata form; still, what occurs here is unusual by his own practice.

A consequence of the expressive intensity found throughout this quartet is the compression of the four instrumental parts into a narrow registral band, resulting from a high cello part, a low first violin, or a combination of both. At the start of the Allegro con spirito (Example 7.1), the first violin not only jumps frequently below the second, but because of its low compass it must be doubled at the lower octave by the viola rather than by the second violin. A sudden shift to a unison scoring accentuates the beginning of bar 4, and so alters the larger metric pattern; the opening seven-bar group, the first of many irregular phrase constructions, is thus the result of two four-bar phrases elided together.

Example 7.1 Op. 20, No. 3, i, bars 1–7

The first and second groups are connected by a transition that is modelled bar for bar on the opening phrase; while the model ends conclusively in G minor, the transition ends on F, the dominant of the new key. But instead of beginning with a theme that is anchored firmly on B♭ in the bass, Haydn recasts the opening idea above a dominant pedal (see Example 7.2a). The advantages of this procedure are twofold: first, the abrupt modulation to the relative major, though never in doubt, is stretched out a little longer by the withholding of the new tonic; second, Haydn is able to redesign the opening theme of the movement in yet another, more affirmative way (Example 7.2b). Neither of these melodies is an exact copy of the original theme: Example 7.2a retains the upper neighbor-note figure, Example 7.2b restores the d^2 on the first downbeat.

Example 7.2 Op. 20, No. 3, i, (a) bars 15–18

(b) Bars 27–30

It would be an exaggeration to say that this movement is monothematic, despite the clear links between bars 1, 15, and 27. Nevertheless, all subsequent new thematic material emerges in the middle of phrases: the high solo violin warbling at bar 34, the antiphonal duets at bar 45, and the first violin's expressive solo on the A string. The use of thematically isolated gestures at the beginning of phrases contributes to a sense that the exposition is the result almost of improvisation.

To establish the home key at the start of the piece, Haydn merely uses a seven-bar phrase with a strong perfect cadence; the relative major, by contrast, is stretched out over nearly seventy bars. Now, it is not unusual for Haydn's sonata form expositions to be built from first and second groups of discrepant sizes, particularly those in minor keys, but the Allegro con spirito is an extreme case, and it is interesting to see how he fashions a long second group, one that fails to make a single full perfect cadence, that is, a V–I progression in B♭ ending with b♭^{1} in the top voice. Crucial to the overarching form of his second group are the two deceptive cadences. The first of these (bar 60) inaugurates a series of gestures in contrasting dynamics, ranging from *forte* to *fortissimo* to *pianissimo* in the space of eight bars. The second (bar 85) is the culmination of the last extended cadential preparation: the diversion to VI means that the harmony never reaches a resting point in B♭.

Example 7.3 outlines the last part of the exposition, after the first deceptive cadence, and gives further illustration of Haydn's cadence construction. The dominant in bars 61–63 resolves to a first-inversion tonic at *(a)*, which moves chromatically to a subdominant chord, on which the violin solo begins, as if in midstream, at *(b)*. Eventually a dominant is reached, at *(c)*, but being built upon the same bass note, it is pulled back to a first-inversion tonic at *(d)*. The drive towards a cadence gains new strength when the bass is lowered an octave, and this time succeeds in reaching the dominant, but now it is thwarted by another interrupted cadence, *(e)*. A repeat of bars 79–81 restores the subdominant, at *(f)*, but here it is too late to cadence in the relative major: the chromatic progression above leads to an augmented sixth chord which irreversibly leads the harmony to its starting point of G minor.

Example 7.3 Op. 20, No. 3, i, outline of bars 61–94

To the irregular phrase construction and continuous thwarting of a cadence is added another feature of the movement, the interpolation of brief, striking gestures that stand out texturally and dynamically from the surrounding material. The first of these gestures, bracketed in Example 7.4, returns five times, and by its frequent appearance is able to compete with the first theme and its variants for motivic prominence. Its interruptive function is clear: the F major chord in bar 24 must wait an additional two bars before resolving to B♭ major and resuming the *forte* dynamic.[2] Appearing almost as an afterthought to bars 15–23, it extends by a further two bars a phrase that is already irregular in design.

Example 7.4 Op. 20, No. 3, i, bars 20–28

The same interpolation, which gives up two sixteenth notes to make space for a rest, is used to opposite purposes towards the end of the exposition.

Instead of prolonging a dominant in the manner of a harmonic echo, it now initiates a phrase on the tonic, as a rescue operation following the deceptive cadence
at bar 85 (see *(e)* in Example 7.3, above). As the alignment of music in Example
7.5 shows, there is a clear analogy with the interruptive figure in bars 77–79
following the violin solo. Only the dynamics are different: *forte* for the broken
chord and trill, *poco piano* for the linear figure.

Example 7.5 Op. 20, No. 3, i, bars 75–90

In the development section, the interpolation is used alongside the main theme
of the piece, but has a more disruptive effect. After establishing D minor by
insisting on its dominant, Haydn quotes it at its original pitch, returning the harmony to B♭ as at bar 27 (compare Example 7.6 with Example 7.4). The juxtaposition of D minor and B♭ major has a destabilizing effect on the harmony, initiating
a cycle of thirds that leads far afield: d–B♭–g–E♭–c–A♭. At the same time, the
shape of the theme at bar 15 is conflated with the texture at the beginning of the
piece (compare with Example 7.1 and Example 7.2).

The central section of the development is a reprise of parts of the second group,
joined together and transposed up a fourth to E♭. The return towards G minor
starts in bar 141 as a simple transposition of bar 110 and the following bars up a
fourth; progress is halted twice by the interpolation, the second of which is
reduced to just two sixteenth notes and two eighths. The effect of these interrup-
tions, which anticipate the late quartets of Beethoven, is not only to prolong the
development by a further seven bars but also to give the illusion almost of two

Example 7.6 Op. 20, No. 3, i, bars 105–111

quartets in competition, through the antiphony between disparate four-part textures established earlier.

Haydn saves some of his greatest surprises for the reprise. To begin with, he anticipates the return to G minor by a bar, thus diffusing some of the energy harnessed in the previous ten bars. After a literal repetition of the main theme, the counterstatement invites the cello to imitate the first violin and then to take over the leadership of the ensemble; hints of an early second-group theme lead to the angular augmented sixths of development (compare bars 103–6 with bars 194–97) and a recomposition of the middle of the second group, all in preparation for the recapitulation of the first violin solo.

Not only does this solo expand the parallel passages in the exposition, from a seven-bar elaboration of a $IV-V_2^4$ progression to a fifteen-bar theme, but its underlying harmonies—the Neapolitan sixth at bar 220, the augmented sixth at bar 225—review, or preview, the most striking harmonic events in the movement. Haydn again dissipates the energy created by this solo in stages, for instance, by the deceptive cadence at bar 242 and the subsequent two-bar interpolation. Then he adds a new phrase, built on the chord of the Neapolitan sixth above the cello's open C string, a sonority more powerful than any yet heard.[3]

The coda, extracts of which are given in Example 7.7, ties together three thematic ideas: the introductory chromatic slide, at *(a)*, itself a recollection of the end of the development; the main theme, at *(b)*; and the original parallel thirds accompaniment of this theme, at *(c)*. The changes of texture following this climax convey a sense of decay: the theme loses its viola doubling and is eventually pared to a solo cello as the dynamics shift down to *pianissimo*. After the instruments regroup in the final diminished seventh chord, the first violin can manage one more outburst before the movement expires quietly on a perfect cadence.

Finally, a word about the key of D minor at the start of the development. In the music of the late eighteenth century, the second group of sonata form movements invariably proceeds in the relative major (III). Of the ten first movements of

Example 7.7 Op. 20, No. 3, i, (a) bars 248–53

(b) Bars 259–64

Haydn quartets set in minor keys, all but two start the development either in the subdominant (iv) or in the submediant (VI). The Allegro innocentemente of Op. 42 turns back to the tonic before moving sequentially through a variety of keys (this occurs frequently in the major). For Op. 20, No. 3, however, Haydn starts the development with the opening theme recast in the minor dominant, a choice that, so far as I am aware, is not made anywhere else in his instrumental works. Despite its rarity, though, there is something archaic about the relationship between i and v: it was the clear preference for binary movements in the Baroque period. And by modifying the original shape of the theme (see Example 7.8), Haydn makes the start of the second half of the movement a "tonal answer" to the opening, thus underscoring the link to an earlier era and alluding to the fugal interest of the Op. 20 set in general.

Example 7.8 Op. 3, No. 3, i, (a) bars 1–4, first violin

(b) Bars 95–98, first violin

MENUET: ALLEGRETTO

The minuet starts like the Allegro con spirito, with the first violin accompanied by parallel thirds in contrary motion. Despite an early climax on a dissonant chord, in bar 4, the overall character of the movement seems less aggressive, partly because the phrases are either of regular length (four or eight bars) or symmetrically paired (five plus five), and partly because the prevailing trio sonata texture is not unbalanced by a doubling of the melody at the octave. The viola plays a minor role, participating where it is needed to flesh out the harmony to four parts.

The central section, made up of a six-bar sequence and two eight-bar phrases, shows us Haydn's sensitivity to changes of texture (see Example 7.9a). The essentially trio-sonata texture can be seen at *(a)*, where the viola, as harmonic filler, contributes to an already dense texture: four parts are confined to the space of an octave. At *(b)* the first violin and cello pause on the dominant, allowing the inner parts to take over the quarter-note movement and leading to a climax at *(c)*, in which all four instruments are active in opposing pairs. The three-part cadence at *(d)*, in which the viola doubles the cello in unison, should not be viewed as an archaism, that is, a reversion to Haydn's quasi-orchestral treatment of the lower strings, but rather is motivated by what follows: the B♭ unison at bar 24 *(e)* provides a more effective gateway to the subsequent unfolding of the mediant chord (B♭–G–E♭) than a fully written-out cadence onto a B♭ chord. For if the viola were to resolve independently through the seventh above the dominant, as hypothesized in Example 7.9b, its final d^1 would not match the starting note in the imitative passage that follows.

Example 7.9 Op. 20, No. 3, ii, (a) bars 11–24

(b) Bars 23–27, with altered viola

In the recapitulation, the modified trio-sonata texture returns, with the viola contributing to the harmony without having a line of its own. The coda, unusually marked *perdendosi*, contains a new twist: the viola remains the "extra" part, but by its rhythmic association with the violins it creates a special low-register antiphony with the cello (see the brackets in Example 7.10). It is as though the viola were, and at the same time were not, an independent voice in the argument.

Example 7.10 Op. 20, No. 3, ii, bars 45–52

The appoggiatura f^2 in bar 4 will probably strike the listener as a sharp dissonance of local significance. When the same f^2 reappears five bars later, however, as part of a $^6_4$ chord in the same rhythmic position, it acquires "thematic" status: what was initially an embellishment of the dominant seventh, f^2–$e\flat^2$–d^2, has now become a cadential progression, f^2–$e\natural^2$–d^2. Identifying bars 9–10 with bars 4–5 makes it easier for the listener to connect these descending thirds with quarter-note descents elsewhere: in the transitional section, for instance, the notes that open the second half of the minuet match the full cadence at bars 23–24 (see Example 7.9, above).

The final reminiscences of f^2–$e\flat^2$-d^2, in the coda, help to explain why Haydn ends the minuet in G major, with a *tierce de Picardie*. The outline in Example 7.11 shows how the motive is brought down an octave and subsumed within the larger descent of a fourth, g^1–f^1–$e\flat^1$–d^1. In keeping with the sombre mood of the passage, Haydn takes the quietest harmonic route through the linear fourth by making f^1 the seventh of a secondary dominant, allowing this note to attach itself gently to $e\flat^1$ and so enhance the plagal quality of the ending.

Example 7.11 Op. 20, No. 3, ii, outline of minuet

One further detail merits attention: the *fortissimo* outburst that consumes itself at the end of the Allegro con spirito (Example 7.12a) covers the sixth from D to B♭, which is the same interval that begins the minuet (Example 7.12b). At first the relationship between them may seem tenuous: the sixths are in different

Example 7.12 Op. 20, No. 3, (a) i, bars 266–70

(b) ii, bars 1–2

c) ii, bars 31–34

registers, and one is a leap while the other filled in by step. But as Haydn leads up to the recapitulation (see Example 7.12c), he fills in the sixth with the same linear progression, and by marking it *con forza* he strengthens the association: the first violin, once again, anticipates the other instruments dynamically.

In six of Haydn's string quartets, the trio section of the minuet or scherzo movement is an incomplete musical structure: instead of writing a trio with two balanced halves, the repetition of which enhances thematic and tonal symmetry, he ends the second part of the trio inconclusively, and the listener expects the return of the minuet to provide the appropriate resolution. The works in question are Op. 9, No. 1, Op. 17, Nos. 2 and 5, and Op. 20, Nos. 1, 2, and 3, all of which date from the period of highly concentrated quartet writing betwen 1769 and 1772.

In three of these movements, the trio ends on the dominant of the home key, and the beginning of the minuet provides a clear and unproblematic resolution. The trio of Op. 17, No. 2, is unusual because it ends on the dominant of its own key, D minor, but this key is closely related to that of the minuet, F major, and the juxtaposition of the two harmonies follows a well-established eighteenth-century tradition. Haydn strengthens the connection between the two sections by tying over the last note of the trio to the starting note of the minuet (Example 7.13).[4]

Example 7.13 Op. 17, No. 2, ii, bars 59–62 followed by reprise of bars 1–2

In the other two quartets, however, the minuet does not provide a straightforward harmonic resolution to the end of the trio. In Op. 20, No. 1, the harmony jumps straight from V/ii to the tonic; this progression will be discussed in chapter 9. The trio of Op. 20, No. 3, set in the submediant key of E♭, is steered off course in the second half: the G major chord on which it ends is unmistakably a *dominant* of C minor, but this dominant is rudely brushed aside by the G minor *tonic* of the return of the minuet (Example 7.14).

Example 7.14 Op. 20, No. 3, ii, bars 77–88 followed by reprise of bars 1–2

The problem here has been summarized by Hans Keller in the following way: "The last thing you expect after the G major chord is G minor, since the G major chord has had dominant function."[5] That is, a cadence may be deceptive in that the dominant moves to some unexpected chord; in other words, the bass moves somewhere other than down a fifth or up a fourth. Here, though, the bass doesn't move anywhere: it just sits on G and exchanges a minor third for a major one.

Can this have been a mistake on Haydn's part? If so, might the trio once have been intended for a different minuet? The ideal partner for a trio beginning in E♭ and ending on the dominant of C would, of course, be a minuet in C minor, which we would only expect to find in a quartet in C minor. Haydn's only C minor quartet, Op. 17, No. 4, is a chronological neighbor of Op. 20, No. 3, and a plausible site for an inconclusive trio in E♭. But the actual minuet of Op. 17, No. 4, is in C major, with a C minor trio (this is a pairing he repeated on two later occasions). That his original plans might have included a minuet in C minor seems unlikely, given the smooth transition to C major in the coda of the previous movement (Example 7.15).

Example 7.15 Op. 17, No. 4, i, bars 127–130 followed by ii, bars 1–4

The other possibility for a logical *progression* from the trio back to the minuet would be for the return of the minuet to enable us to hear the G major ending of the trio retrospectively as a tonic, by actually including a progression from V/IV (G major) to IV (C minor). Such a progression is indeed found in the minuet, but it occurs at the very end of the movement. While it may be possible to imagine the connection, that is, to imagine the first part of Example 7.14 followed by Example 7.10, it seems unlikely that Haydn intended the listener to suspend perception of harmonic events during the intervening forty-four bars.[6]

Unless we are to infer a tonal miscalculation here, we must accept that there is, after all, no connection between the end of the trio and the da capo, and Haydn has, uniquely, written a minuet in G minor that ends *conclusively* in G major (as a tonic with raised third), followed by a trio in E♭ that ends *inconclusively* in G major (as a dominant). The da capo is necessary for the proportions of the movement, but it is not sufficient to resolve the concluding harmony of the trio; the sections remain unconnected. A performance that accepts this uncoupling will, I think, have to make the ending of the trio sound very relaxed, with a pause before the da capo: Haydn's extra bar of rest suggests as much. A slight emphasis of the first violin's neighbor-note figures, for instance, by the slurring of g^1–f♯^{1}–g^1 in bars 83–86, may render the status of G major less clear-cut.[7]

POCO ADAGIO

In his brief remarks on Op. 20, No. 3, for the "Haydn" entry in *Cobbett's Cyclopedic Survey of Chamber Music*, Tovey blamed the critical failure of the work on its slow movement, "which has a breadth not easily distinguished from length by spoilt modern audiences."[8] To be sure, it is much the longest Haydn quartet slow movement to date: 113 bars in 3/4 time, of which 43 are marked to be repeated. Tovey attributed the tempo marking of "Poco adagio," rather than just "Adagio," to Haydn's possible unease about the movement's exceptional length. This is an interesting anachronism: while performances seventy years ago might have paid scant attention to the adverbial qualification, current practice is more likely to make a distinction between the tempo of this movement and that of comparably paced movements in 3/4 time, such as the Largo of Op. 9, No. 5, the Largo cantabile of Op. 54, No. 3, and the Adagio of Op. 64, No. 5.

While the extended focus on the cello (e.g. in bars 13–22) is an important innovation, the most interesting textures are those in which the roles initially established for the outer parts (first violin = solo melody, cello = fastest moving part) are reversed. Haydn achieves this in the long development section, first successively, then simultaneously. In the first of these passages (Example 7.16a), the cello reshapes the melody in order to stay within a comfortable range. The second passage is more problematic, on account of the registral limitation of the viola; in the middle section (Example 7.16b), the natural tenor range of the melodic cello, together with the unavailability of a bass B (the viola's lower limit is its open C), results in bunching of lines: in bars 70–71 and again in bars 74–75, the second violin arpeggio crosses both below the bass and above the melody.

Example 7.16 Op. 20, No. 3, iii, (a) bars 51–56

(b) Bars 74–79

Extreme compression of part-writing seems, in fact, to have been a feature of this movement from the outset, when Haydn drafted the opening four bars as a cello solo (Example 7.17). Difficulties in working out a suitable four-part harmony may be one reason why he did not complete the passage. After altering the third bar of the bass line (taken by the viola) to accommodate the first-violin inner part, he simply left the second violin blank in bars 3–4. Yet it is hard to imagine that he was satisfied with less than full four-part harmony here.

Example 7.17 Haydn's draft of Op. 20, No. 3, iii, bars 1–4

The final version also has the advantage in setting up the cello as *a different kind of solo instrument* after the opening twelve-bar exposition. It also means the first violin can be heard later, to great advantage, as *appropriating the cello part* (bars 23–24, 55ff., 72ff.), and the cello doing the same in return (bars 51–54, 70ff.).

If in the first movement Haydn dares to extend his second group to a considerable length, he does so again here, with great skill. The slow-movement sketch (Example 7.18a) is instructive once more, for it shows the violin solo climaxing with a deceptive cadence. (The fermata on the $^6_4$ chord probably indicates a short cadenza.) In the final version (Example 7.18b), by contrast, the deceptive cadence and the climax of the violin solo are separated by three full bars. What is more, the troublesome B minor chord returns after the climax, now as part of the closing group harmony. The submediant has an entirely new function here: it allows the harmony to pass smoothly from the resumption of D major to a subdominant (G) stretched over ten bars. The repeat of the B minor chord thus helps Haydn to join together two D major periods into an almost seamless group of twenty-two bars.

Example 7.18 Op. 20, No. 3, iii, (a) Haydn's sketch of bars 30–32, first violin and cello

The *bariolage* in the codetta, the alternation of stopped and open strings in bars 41–42, is a technique found in Haydn's earliest quartets (see chapter 2). In a wonderful reversal, the d^1, which represents the key note of the second group, becomes a dominant pedal in the lead-in to the recapitulation (Example 7.19). Not only does the extended *bariolage* connect the end of the development to the recapitulation, it is itself a development of the second violin's held note in the

(b) Final version, bars 25–32

second group, bars 19–22, and thus makes a recapitulation of this passage unnecessary.

Example 7.19 Op. 20, No. 3, iii, bars 84–92

FINALE: ALLEGRO DI MOLTO

The Allegro di molto, a short sonata-form movement, synthesizes elements of the first two movements of the quartet. The opening theme modifies that of the minuet, but the most important rhythmic pattern, four sixteenth notes plus two eighths, was also a conspicuous feature of the Allegro con spirito. In the outer movements, too, the paired opposition of the upper and lower instruments, in parallel thirds, provides an important alternative to the textures dominated by the first violin.

Unlike the first movement, however, the finale contains no new motives whose purpose is to disrupt thematic and harmonic development. The abrupt move from G minor to E♭, which starts the transition to the relative major, is achieved by a bar's rest followed by a sudden *forte* (Example 7.20a); the unison figure is a recognizable variation on the opening rhythm. Haydn capitalizes on his earlier insistence upon the V_2^4–I^6 progression (bars 2, 6, and 7), leaving the B♭ to dangle in the bass as the d^2 it supports resolves as a leading note on the next downbeat.

This mildly disruptive effect, created early in the movement, leads Haydn to a more daring harmonic move in the recapitulation (Example 7.20b). The opening phrase has now been extended to C minor which, taken at face value, is more closely related to E♭ major in bar 80. But because C minor was reached via its leading note, B♭ and B♮ are in conflict in the bass; this conflict is not compensated for by a smooth progression in the melody. The greatest surprise, though, is yet to come: the C♭ in bar 81 at once negates both the chord of C minor and the leading note B♮.

Example 7.20 Op. 20, No. 3, iv, (a) bars 11–15

(b) Bars 75–82

One further detail is worthy of attention, the inversion of parts at the beginning of the movement to produce the distinctive texture of the codetta. The initial leap from a^1 to d^2 (Example 7.21a) is easily explained as an interval within a single chord, namely, the dominant of G. When transferred to the bass, the harmony becomes ambiguous. It is possible to hear the cello in Example 7.21b as a B♭ pedal embellished by its lower fourth; in context, however, the leaps are more likely to sound like V–I progressions in B♭. This ambiguity is exploited in the recapitulation, where Haydn extends the codetta by embellishing the harmony with V–I progressions in the subdominant (Example 7.21c). The extended harmony is still well served by a tonic pedal (see the analysis in Example 7.21d), but the ambiguity of the earlier passage is thrown into confusion by the persistence of the fourth, D–G.

Example 7.21 Op. 20, 3, iv, (a) bars 1–2

(b) Bars 38–42

(c) Bars 98–104

(d) Outline of bars 98–104

Against the V^7–I progressions in C minor, the fourths bracketed in Example 7.21c can be understood only as an embellishment of the upper note, G, since the D has no part to play in a C minor chord. Yet the interval continues to enjoy an equivocal status elsewhere in the passage, where the upper parts plot V–I (or V–I$^{\natural 3}$) progressions in G minor. Thus the finale closes on an ambiguous note, which is somehow emblematic of a work that, for all its power of expression, continues to hold many mysteries.

8

Quartet in D Major, Op. 20, No. 4

If the C major quartet best represents Haydn's achievements among the works in Op. 20 that end with a fugue, then it is probably the D major that most fully represents the composer's achievements in the other subset of this opus, the three quartets whose finales are in sonata form. The long and richly developed first movement is replete with interesting textures and string-playing techniques. The slow movement develops the cello as a melodic instrument with due regard for its lower register; the harmonically extended coda breaks new ground in variation form. The Menuet alla Zingarese is an ingenious rhythmic puzzle, to which the first of Haydn's cello-dominated trio sections forms the perfect complement. Finally, the Presto e scherzando pursues elements of the gypsy style that the previous movement, the shortest of all Haydn's quartet minuets, could not accommodate.

ALLEGRO DI MOLTO

The Allegro di molto conforms in its broad outline to Haydn's first-movement sonata forms of the period. Its three principal sections are about the same length: the development is almost as long as the exposition, but a false reprise of the opening theme accounts for a tenth of its length and a corresponding shortening of the recapitulation. The internal organization of the exposition (see Table 8.1), like that of the first movement from the previous quartet, is weighted towards the second group: the opening paragraph in D is just 30 bars long, and the rest of the exposition comprises 82 bars. The latter includes a harmonic transition which, characteristic of movements in major, takes longer to reach the contrasting key: Haydn is aiming for A major by about bar 40, and reaches it several bars later, but he does not actually cadence in A until bar 67. The next part of the second group stays firmly in A major, but goes through a similar developmental process to the first 37 bars: development of the opening theme, virtuoso triplet figurations, slower motion leading to a cadence. The final part of the exposition comprises a closing theme and a codetta, whose interrelations are discussed below.

Table 8.1
Outline of the exposition of Op. 20, No. 4, first movement

Bar	Material
1	first group, comprising five six-bar phrases, beginning and ending in D
	second group: first part
31	modulation to A, via its minor dominant and augmented sixth
47	settling in A major
67	first A major cadence
	second group: second part
68	new cycle of development, beginning with recall of opening theme
83	caesura on V^7/V of A
84	new theme, rounding off harmony in A major
87	second A major cadence
89	counterstatement of new theme
99	third A major cadence
	second group: third part
99	closing theme, with further A major cadences
107	codetta
112	return to beginning, or shift up to B (later as V of E minor)

The movement begins with three quarter notes and a dotted half note, all on the same pitch, out of which develops a six-bar phrase (Example 8.1). This is a classic example of what I called an "ideal" theme in chapter 2, since a series of repeated notes lends itself to virtually unlimited variation by any member of the ensemble. The progress of the opening tune is from short notes to long notes and back to short ones; the bass encapsulates this by starting and ending with quarter notes and holding on to a D pedal throughout the intervening four bars.

In identifying Example 8.1 as an "ideal" theme, I am not implying that catchy tunes and beautiful melodies are less suitable to development or imaginative part-writing, but it is the composer's task to work out the implications of that material. Here, by contrast, thematic development is *impossible to avoid*, since the principal theme is made up of the simplest elements: a single note moving at a steady pulse.

In the first paragraph, which comprises five six-bar phrases, we can see the

Example 8.1 Op. 20, No. 4, i, bars 1–6

repeated note developed in several ways, for instance, by the linear joining of the dominant to the tonic (cello, bars 11–12), and by the tonic broken chord in the bass at the first perfect cadence (viola and cello, bars 29–30). Even a different articulation of the repeated notes constitutes a kind of development: the *portato* beginning befits the expressive qualities of a thematic incipit, but the lower strings end the phrase with detached notes, as is appropriate for a bass-note pedal (see Example 8.1).[1]

Of course, the very simplicity of the opening is also a test of Haydn's inventiveness: if everything originates in a single note, then the shaping of a musical argument, including the derivation of new ideas from old ones, becomes as much a challenge as the designing of a more "substantial" theme. Haydn continues the long process of thematic development in this movement by extending the repeated quarter notes to other rhythmic levels. At the start of the transition (Example 8.2), one can hear the arpeggio triplets as a variation on the repeated-note theme: here, of course, the repetition of the note B occurs in different octaves.

Example 8.2 Op. 20, No. 4, i, bars 31–36

The identification of repeated quarter notes and arpeggios in triplets leads in turn to more general forms of triplet embellishment, though there are sufficient reminders of the original broken chord (cello in bars 44, 46; first violin in bar 47). In fact, the powers of motivic identification in a diversity of material are so great that a genuinely contrasting thematic idea—a new theme—does not emerge until bar 84, after a dramatically abrupt halt on an A^7 chord (Example 8.3). Here the quartet parts are paired off, with the thirds in the treble and bass used in antiphonal opposition, a perfect complement to the earlier emphasis on four-part unisons and solo virtuosity.

Example 8.3 Op. 20, No. 4, i, bars 82–91

The closing theme synthesizes two features of earlier themes that had previously been kept separate: triplet rhythms, and the pairing of voices in thirds. The counterstatement of this theme inverts both the order of the parts and the direction of the lines. The turns that round off each phrase of the closing theme, one the one hand, reduce the preceding triplet figure from five notes to four (compare *(a)* and *(b)* in Example 8.4), and on the other, recall the opening theme of the movement (Example 8.1, bars 5–6). This connection helps Haydn to link the closing theme to the codetta, which starts off with a turn. But since the turn figure is part of the opening theme, the repeated quarter notes that follow (Example 8.4, at *(c)*) bring us back smoothly to the opening of the movement.

The development is the longest of any Haydn quartet before the 1790s, its 103 bars nearly equalling the length of the exposition. Its course follows the thematic pattern of the exposition by emphasizing, in turn, the main theme, triplet figurations, and the closing theme. Although the harmony stays in keys closely related to D, the development divides naturally into four subsections, as shown in Table 8.2. Of special interest are the two false reprises: a literal quotation of the start of

Example 8.4 Op. 20, No. 4, i, bars 101–9

the movement, and a transposition of this theme to G major some ten bars before the definitive return of the home key.

Table 8.2

Outline of the development section of Op. 20, No. 4, first movement

Bar	Material
113–147	development of main theme, from dominant of E minor to dominant of B minor; includes quotation of the opening (bars 133–138)
148–187	triplet figuration developed in long passage beginning and ending in B minor
187–204	development of closing theme, ending in B major as the dominant of E minor
(205)	(general pause)
206–215	preparation for recapitulation, with main theme transposed to G

The outline of the harmony of bars 113–148, given in Example 8.5, shows that tonal tension is maintained by a sequence of pedals, most of them suggesting the dominants of keys that do not fully materialize. The intensity is heightened by the insertion of chromatic passing notes between the pedals, but the effect is broken at the arrival on D, the tonic of the movement, whereupon Haydn brings back the opening theme in its original form (only the *portato* articulations of bar 1 are missing). This distinctive event is also signalled by a change of register, and points to Haydn's use throughout the development section of a high-register bass for tonally active sections, whereas the low-register bass is associated with the harmonic stasis of the main theme.

Example 8.5 Op. 20, No. 4, i, outline of bars 113–48

The timing and preparation of D major hardly suggests that the recapitulation is at hand in bar 133, but the emergence of the opening points the way towards its return in the subdominant, G major, seventy-three bars later. The later event, the movement's "true" false reprise, sets up the real return of the main theme, in D major, ten bars later; it also enables Haydn to shorten the five phrases of the movement's opening paragraph to three.

Although tonal exploration is not one of its striking characteristics, the development exhibits some well-planned changes in harmonic rhythm. As a comparison of Example 8.6 with Example 8.2 will show, the section starts in the same key and with the same texture found at the start of the transition to the second group. The virtuosity of the solo part is, of course, enhanced by continuous triplet motion, replacing the stopping and starting of the transition, but the harmony is prevented from changing more than once every two bars at *(a)*; by the end of the passage, at *(b)*, there is a chord change in every bar. The progress to a faster pattern is subtly aided by the triplet figures themselves as they move from a two-bar to a one-bar pattern in bars 154–155, that is, *before* the change of harmonic rhythm; the faster chord changes, in turn, encourage a more animated triplet figuration from bar 156, with a new pattern built on three notes instead of nine (see the square brackets in the first violin part).

Following a brief intervention of the main theme, Haydn resumes the development of the triplets at the accelerated harmonic rate. From here to the end, the development focuses on texture and the distribution of interest among the parts, starting with the second violin triplets (bars 166–172), leading to antiphony between first violin and cello (bars 173–176), and finally offering a cello solo (bars

Example 8.6 Op. 20, No. 4, i, bars 148–59

177–180), whose momentum is increased by an accelerated chord change for the cycle of fifths leading to B minor.

Apart from shortening the opening paragraph and omitting the modulation, the recapitulation follows the exposition in nearly all details. The codetta, however, has been recomposed for the formal repeat, and so reinforces the circular thematic process in the exposition. Now the tonic pedal drops out sooner, so that the turn figure can be heard to fall back upon the repeated quarter notes. The reduced dynamics in the second ending, from *forte* to *piano* to *pianissimo*, provide a further link with the beginning of the movement. The final gesture (Example 8.7) completes the circle left open by the first six-bar phrase: the turn-figure, originally played by the violins in parallel thirds, is recalled literally in bars 295–296 of the second ending, and descends sequentially before melting into the opening motive.

Example 8.7 Op. 20, No. 4, i, bars 295b–98b

As explained in chapter 2, open strings give the string quartet extra resonance, and they usually feature in loud passages. In this movement, however, their two prominent occurrences are, exceptionally, associated with *pianissimo*. In bar 25, the C♮ unison in the four parts follows a deflection of the harmony to B minor, and represents the intersection of the descending melody and the rising bass (see the arrows in Example 8.8). It is also the first nonharmonic note in the piece, and its contextually eerie quality is reinforced by the cold C strings of the viola and cello, as these notes can only be performed without vibrato.[2]

Example 8.8 Op. 20, No. 4, i, outline of bars 21–26

The reprise at bar 206 (Example 8.9a) is false in two senses: G major is neither the home key of the piece, nor is it the correct resolution of the previous chord, the dominant of E minor. Here only the violins are actually obliged to play their low note on the open G, yet the character of the passage should encourage the viola and cello to do the same, which in turn will throw into sharper relief the high G major chord that starts the next phrase (Example 8.9b).

Example 8.9 Op. 20, No. 4, i, (a) bars 206–7

(b) Bars 212–15

UN POCO ADAGIO E AFFETTUOSO

Op. 20 was Haydn's first set of quartets not to include a first movement in variation form, and the trend in his quartet writing is away from this practice: of the remaining six sets, only two start with variations (Op. 55, No. 2, and Op.76, No. 6). The opus, is, however, also the first to include a slow-movement variation, a feature that will occur with increasing frequency in later years and lead to a doubling of the average number of variation movements in a set of six works.[3]

The layout of the variations of Op. 20, No. 4, is, superficially, typical of the genre. The theme is a richly accompanied violin solo, and the ensuing variations allow other members of the ensemble to share or take over the principal moving part. The reprise of the original theme after the variations is also a common technique; here, as in Op. 9, No. 5, Haydn tellingly refrains from marking it "variation" in the score.[4] What makes this movement special is, first of all, the intensity of expression in the second half of the theme; second, the participation of the lower instruments in the variations; and finally the extended reprise of the theme. These features will be discussed in turn.

The theme begins in a *galant* manner, with antecedent and consequent phrases setting up bb^1–a^1 in the first violin against g–f in the cello as a contrapuntal frame. In the first phrase (see Example 8.10a), this frame supports a diminished seventh and its resolution back to D minor; in the second (Example 8.10b), it circumscribes a II^7–V–I progression in F major.

Example 8.10 Op. 20, No. 4, ii, (a) bars 1–4

(b) Bars 5–8

In the second half, b♭[1] and g return to mark out a G minor chord, which is pivotal for the return to D minor. An exchange of voices (shown by the crossed lines in Example 8.11) leads smoothly to an augmented sixth and its resolution on the dominant (bars 11–12). The entire procedure is repeated, with the harmonies now stretched to fit the larger, six-bar concluding phrase and each of the upper string parts based on its own sequential pattern against the steadily rising cello line.[5] The harmony is intensified by the 5–6 steps in the viola: the resultant Neapolitan sixth chord in bar 13 will have important resonances in the final reprise of the theme.

Example 8.11 Op. 20, No. 4, ii, outline of bars 9–18

The tension also increases as the melodic line continues to rise, opening up a new space in the last phrase. Haydn lets the second violin take over the a^1 in bar 12, freeing the first violin to explore the higher register (Example 8.12). Deprived of its proper melodic range, however, it can do no better than ornament the rising bass line around the notes g^2–a^2–$b♭^2$. The embellishments minimize the effect of parallel octaves between the outer parts, and the thirty-second-note figures in bars 15–16 give the effect of a fleeting violin duet. Both violins are now aiming to end on the same note, d^2, which is an octave too high for the resolution of the theme as a whole.

Example 8.12 Op. 20, No. 4, ii, bars 11–16

Viewed conventionally, the purpose of the first variation is to animate the rhythm of the theme by giving greater interest to the inner parts of the quartet ensemble. The first violin now belongs to the quiet accompaniment, while the cello plays virtually the same bass line as it had in the theme. (Its articulation is now more *staccato*, to match the other parts.) The second violin thus takes over the melody, and the viola part gains in interest by interacting with the second violin, e.g. by responding to thrity-second-note runs or by imitating its three-note figures in the sequential phrase.

Seen as a continuation of the theme, this variation helps resolve difficulties of part-writing and register discussed earlier. Most obviously, the elimination of the first violin from the argument removes the threat of parallel octaves in bars 31–33. More crucial for the overall planning, however, is the early arrival of the high d^3 in the second half, which is quickly played out, allowing the upbeat to bar 31 to return immediately to the starting point of the melody, a^1 (Example 8.13). From here to the end, the variation follows the part-writing of the theme, and the melody falls back easily onto low d^1. Indeed, the only business the first violin has here is to assist with the four-part German sixth chords in bars 31 and 35. In other words, the important features of the theme—the high d^3, and the rising sequence—are present, but their appearance in reverse order enables the variation to close with the melody in its natural register. Of course, Variation I offers only temporary solutions to the problems of part-writing and register: it creates new expectations, namely, the use of the cello as soloist, and the return of the first violin as the rightful proprietor of the melodic line.

Example 8.13 Op. 20, 4, No. ii, bars 29–32

Variation II introduces the cello as a melodic instrument for the first time in a set of variations by Haydn. But its line is not exclusively a melody: it is a careful weaving of melody, bass, and inner part into a single line, with touches of ambiguity as it moves between these roles. Thus in Example 8.14 the unaccompanied upbeat at *(a)* is a clear sign of a cello melody at the beginning, but the next four notes form an inner part below the violins. Either violin could claim to be the melody here: the first violin is the highest sounding part, though the second violin plays the changing-note figure from the original theme, e^1–f^1–$c\sharp^1$–d^1. Against such competition, the cello needs a grace note at *(b)* to maintain its prominence. The four-part texture breaks off, allowing the cello once again to initiate the action and remain the point of focus. It had left off on A, the root of the dominant chord that follows. By embellishing this with a broad triplet arpeggio, at *(c)*, Haydn gently reminds us of the instrument's traditional bass function. Of course the low A doesn't resolve to a low D, and when the other instruments reenter the viola resumes the bass line. Still, the viola's g–f does not have quite the force to push the cello arpeggio entirely into the background, and the listener is left with the impression of two parts competing for the bass.

Example 8.14 Op. 20, No. 4, ii, bars 37–40

In the second half of the variation, the cello makes its climax early, the grace notes in bar 47 ensuring its predominance before it slips below the first violin. Here Haydn confronts the old problem of a redundant fourth part in the rising sequence, and once again the solution is original: the cello uses arpeggio figures to embellish the bass line and rises above the viola when four-part harmony is required by the German sixth. The variation ends with the cello returning as the inner part of a trio sonata.

The necessity of Variation III is based on the balance among the instruments: the attention given to the lower strings in the previous variations requires a return to the quartet leader as soloist. At the same time, however, the high d^3 in bars 69–70 makes a resolution of the melody in its natural, low register impossible. A simple reprise of the theme at the end of the movement will not solve the main problem of register, the opposition of d^2 to d^1, but an extended continuation allows Haydn to explore harmonic features of the theme and release the tension wound up once more by the rising sequence

This continuation is, to my knowledge, unprecedented in the variation literature, and is of inestimable significance for the history of the variation set. It takes the form of a written-out cadenza, from the $\frac{6}{4}$ chord at the end of the theme to a trill thirty bars later. It unfolds in two harmonic cycles that build up to the bass progression G–G♯–A, a clear reference to the end of the theme. At the beginning of the first cycle, Haydn increases the tension still further by pushing above the original upper boundary of d^3. The interval of a third between the upper parts makes for an easier pairing off of the upper and lower strings. The emerging violin solo embellishes the upper voice of a three-part harmony. The Neapolitan sixth is reached in bar 98, but Haydn extends the sequence by two bars to arrive at a root-position E♭ chord before turning the corner to aim for the first G–G♯–A. The solo violin converts the subdominant into a diminished seventh chord, which is answered with a sudden *fortissimo* by all four instruments in a rhetorical unison.

The second cycle starts with a passage recalling the triplet sixteenth notes of Variation III, and leads to four-part chordal writing reminiscent of the theme. The brief chain of $^6_3$ chords momentarily regains the intensity of the high-register thirds with which the cadenza began; the cello joins in, preparing the support for the next violin arpeggio over G. This time the arpeggio outlines the familiar Neapolitan sixth and, with a reversal of dynamics, the ensuing diminished chord is played *pianissimo*. A deceptive cadence after the trill leads to a IV–V–I cadence.

MENUET ALLA ZINGARESE: ALLEGRETTO

From a contemporary west European perspective, the notion of music "in the gypsy style" is strongly associated with the exotic, that is, with surface characteristics that seem foreign to the basic style of an era. Understanding an eighteenth-century minuet marked *alla Zingarese* is further complicated by our having grown up with late nineteenth-century connotations of the term: the spotlighting of a solo performer (usually a violinist), a tendency towards rhythmic freedom in an improvisatory manner, and a musical scale featuring augmented intervals or additional (or unusually distributed) semitones, capable of generating nondiatonic melodies. These are, to be sure, features of Haydn's "gypsy style," but they are not ones that he exploits here.

The Menuet alla Zingarese, the only quartet movement in which Haydn included a stylistic modifier in the title,[6] is instead concerned with the accentuation of notes other than those falling on the downbeat. This other sense of *alla Zingarese* derives from what had earlier been dubbed the "Hungarian style." The sixteenth-century *ungaresca*, for instance, was a dance in duple meter with a heavily accented melody. Another related term, *alla zoppa* ("limping"), refers to a dislocation of accent, usually from the downbeat to the second eighth note in a moderate 2/4 tempo. In this minuet, Haydn has fitted the parts in such a way that agogic accents might appear on any of the quarter-note beats of the bar and thus throw the phrase rhythm into utter disarray. At one point, there are six such accents in succession, though never in the same part on successive beats and never in all four parts on the same beat. (The *fz* markings can thus be thought of more as cautionary signs, alerting the instrument to the possibility that it may be solely responsible for one of these accents and should not expect support from other parts.)

Although the overall effect is of unpredictable accentuation, Haydn has achieved it by solid technical means. As Hans Keller has demonstrated, the first violin part can be rebarred as a gavotte, alla breve with an upbeat of two quarter notes and without *fz* markings;[7] or, to put it another way, Haydn achieves a comic effect by superimposing one courtly dance pattern upon another. While the second violin follows the gavotte rhythms of the first, the viola and cello provide just enough indication of the underlying minuet. The invitation to hemiola proves irresistible, however, and Haydn obliges with three groups of two beats, conventionally, in the bars immediately preceding the perfect cadences at bars 8 and 20.[8]

As if these rhythmic intricacies weren't sufficient, the return modulation to D major includes an additional complication: the two violins are set in canonic imitation, at a distance of a single quarter note. The instruments are accordingly regrouped: the cello follows the second violin, while the viola is initially aligned with the first violin before acting independently to fill out the harmony. While the canon increases the rhythmic interaction of the parts, the introduction of a new figure of four unstressed eighth notes prevents accents from falling on every beat.

The marking *alla Zingarese* applies only to the rhythm: there are no augmented or diminished intervals, or any other evidence—yet!—of a harmonically based gypsy style. Nevertheless, the phrase compression that gives the cross-accents their wit also confuses the tonality. As can be seen in Example 8.15a, the first violin outlines a dominant seventh in D major (marked *a*), which, instead of resolving to a tonic, moves directly to the leading note of A. Haydn amusingly capitalizes on the clash between $g\natural^2$ and $g\sharp^1$ by constantly reiterating the three-note cadential figure (marked *b*) that contains the leading-note resolution ($g\sharp^1$–e^1–a^1). The second half corrects the harmonic "mistake" of the opening (see Example 8.15b): the same arpeggiated dominant seventh chord now contains the correct leading note, so that motives *a* and *b* now overlap.

Menuet alla Zingarese
Allegretto

Example 8.15 Op. 20, No. 4, iii, (a) Bars 2–6, first violin

(b) Bars 15–18, first violin

The trio, which uses simple harmonies in the simplest possible phrase structure, is the perfect foil to the Menuet alla Zingarese. Its chief interest lies in the emphasis on the cello: though its role in articulating the bass line is undisputed, its faster movement gives the effect of an inversion of the texture. The paradoxical situation of a single part owning both the melodic and the harmonic interest is broken only in the middle four bars of this miniature a–a'–b–a form: when the first violin joins the cello with a line of eighth notes, the viola's pedal A assumes the bass.[9]

PRESTO E SCHERZANDO

While it is unthinkable that a Classical composer would write two consecutive movements in the same exotic style, the last movement of this quartet completes the gypsy program begun in the minuet. Chromatic melodies appear and, despite a well-integrated quartet style exploring various homophonic and contrapuntal textures, the first violin regains the spotlight as soloist. The gypsy style is most marked in the closing theme (see Example 8.16), with its slurred octave leaps; off-beat accents, including *acciaccature*; and the likely use of open A strings by three of the instruments. Haydn's two kinds of *staccato* marking here, the dot and the wedge, offer further evidence of an airy execution that is appropriate to the lighter style.[10]

Example 8.16 Op. 20, No. 4, iv, bars 40–43

The distribution and development of themes need not be examined in great detail. The main theme (Example 8.17a) is made up of a bouncy figure for solo violin, *a,* and the chromatic step motive, *b.* If these two components seem tacked together, that is partly because the fast notes precede the slow notes, the reverse of what we normally find in Classical themes, and partly because Haydn develops them as separate ideas. The transition to the dominant (see Example 8.17b) is based entirely on the chromatic motive. It is developed sequentially, then reduced from three quarter notes to two eighths:

Example 8.17 Op. 20, No. 4, iv, (a) bars 1–2

(b) Bars 13–16

The second group (Example 8.18a) starts by developing the solo figure, first by canonic entries at *(a)*, later by extending the sixteenth-note motive into a longer arpeggiation figure, at *(b)*. Haydn builds up to the climax of the exposition by playing the violin figure and the chromatic motive against each other, in a pair of interlocking duets (Example 8.18b).

Example 8.18 Op. 20, No. 4, iv, (a) bars 19–22

(b) Bars 33–34

The melodic gypsy style in the Presto e scherzando originates not in the chromatic step motive, but in a new theme that mixes elements of D minor and A major (Example 8.19a). That the perfect fourth in bar 7 becomes a diminished fourth in bar 8 is not in itself remarkable, but Haydn crucially delays the resolution of the leading note $c\sharp^2$ by interpolating a short violin solo on the diminished fourth. Together with the earlier neighbor-note figure, a^2–$g\sharp^2$–a^2, the violin solo delineates the exotic scale given in Example 8.19b.

Example 8.19 Op. 20, No. 4, iv, (a) bars 7–11

(b) Elements of "gypsy scale"

In the recapitulation, the exoticism of F♮ is strengthened by a reference to the closing subject added to the gypsy theme. But there is an intermediate stage in the transformation of bar 40 into bar 90: the final part of the development section is activated by a new variant, which reduces the essentials of the closing subject to the space of two bars. The full thematic development is illustrated in Example 8.20.

Example 8.20 Op. 20, No. 4, iv, (a) bar 40

(b) Bars 70–71

(c) Bars 88–91

9

Quartet in E♭ Major, Op. 20, No. 1

If the E♭ quartet was intended to conclude Op. 20, it certainly cannot claim to be its climax. On the contrary, a preference for flat keys, low registers, note values of moderate length, and *legato* articulation makes this quartet the most subdued in the cycle. It contains little in the way of virtuoso artistry and little of the drama normally associated with sonata style, apart from a mildly surprising move to B♭ minor in the minuet and a *fortissimo* outburst midway through the finale. An unrepresentative product of Haydn's so-called *Sturm und Drang* period, Op. 20, No. 1, is more likely to reach us through the intellect than through the viscera. Tovey, writing in Great Britain in 1929, described it as a work "unknown to concert-goers" and likely to appeal to the musical equivalent of "connoisseurs of T'ang china."[1]

At the same time, Op. 20, No. 1, enjoys a certain reputation as a model for quartet writing in the Classical period. Beethoven made a copy of it around 1793; and while none of his chamber works has been shown to be overtly influenced by it, the motivic richness and textual variety of Haydn's quartet style of the early 1770s informs much of Beethoven's chamber music output up to the Op. 18 quartets. More specfic is the connection with Mozart: the Affettuoso e sostenuto is widely accepted as having a direct influence on the slow movement of K. 428 in E♭, the third of the six quartets dedicated to Haydn in 1785;[2] that these quartets were, by their composer's own admission, the product of a "long, laborious effort" and not dashed off with his legendary aplomb, further suggests the importance of Haydn's quartet as a model.

ALLEGRO MODERATO

The very opening of the first movement, with its trio-sonata texture in a low register, forecasts an intimacy that is characteristic of the entire quartet. Yet in spite of the emphasis on small groupings in the opening paragraph (full, idiomatic four-part quartet writing is not heard until the half cadence in bars 14–15, almost halfway through the exposition) the Allegro moderato offers a virtually complete catalogue of 18th-century quartet textures: trio-sonata passages, duets in all six possible combinations of the instruments, antiphonally paired duets (in all three possible combinations), rhetorical unisons, accompanied and unaccompanied violin solos, and rich four-part scoring. Haydn is no less aware here of the contrapuntal potential of the four instruments than he is in the most intricate passages of his fugal finales.

Where this movement stands apart is in its pacing. None of the other first movements of Op. 20 nor any of the fugal finales proceeds quite so leisurely as this Allegro moderato. The first paragraph follows the tonal design of a fugue, with statements of the main theme in the tonic (bar 1), dominant (bar 7), and again the tonic (bar 11). But where a fugal answer is indeed a response to the subject and a direct challenge to its tonal authority, the B♭ statement of the opening theme is the outcome of a two-bar modulation in which the original key has been left behind (Example 9.1). Of course, this is not the real modulation to the dominant such as we expect in a sonata form, but we do not know this in bar 7, when the new key arrives on the scene.

Example 9.1 Op. 20, No. 1, i, bars 4–7

In the transition to the second group, solo passages for the first violin stretch out the crucial harmonic progressions. The chromatic sequence in bars 16–19, which reinterprets E♭ major as IV of B♭, could easily be accommodated in half the space. The I^6–IV–V–I cadential progression that affirms B♭ major as the new key in bar 28 is expanded by further solo music that, instead of developing material presented earlier, proceeds in the manner of a cadenza (Example 9.2a). The angular violin arpeggio in bars 24–25 is similar to the cello solo in the subsequent phrase (Example 9.2b), but it would be wrong to make too much of the resemblance: the violin merely extends the I^6 chord of Bb, whereas the cello is motivically important, helping to maintain sixteenth-note motion across the whole of the phrase to which it belongs and preparing a new theme, for the cello, in bar 32. Haydn, moreover, makes no attempt to show a connection between the on-the-beat, slurred presentation in the violin and the off-the-beat cello figure in detached bowing four bars later.

Example 9.2 Op. 20, No. 1, i, (a) bars 24–25, first violin

(b) Bars 29–30

As is often the case with Haydn's sonata forms, the contrasting key is affirmed nearer the end of the exposition than the middle. The cello melody in bars 32–33 is in effect the "second theme," with one-bar antecedent and consequent phrases and a counterstatement in the higher octave. The "closing theme" (bar 34) is not only ingeniously derived from it—the head-motive from the second theme (Example 9.3a) is transformed into a duet in thirds (Example 9.3b)—but is also linked with the main theme of the piece. When we listen to the repeat of the exposition, we understand why the opening motive (Example 9.3c) is embellished when it returns in Eb as the third entry of the "fugal exposition" (Example 9.3d): the head-motive of the closing theme turns out to be a compressed form of this embellishment.

Example 9.3 Op. 20, No. 1, i, (a) bar 34, first violin

(b) Bar 36, first and second violins

(c) Bar 1, first violin and viola

(d) Bar 11

In order to understand the workings of the development section, it is useful to take a closer look at the opening theme (Example 9.4), whose three-part counterpoint is arranged in the two alternative forms of trio sonata texture: (1) two melodic lines above a bass, and (2) a solo line above two accompanying parts. Both of these forms are slightly "defective" in Haydn's theme. To begin with, the viola supports the violin at the lower third for half a bar; in order to retain the tonic harmony, it jumps at *(a)* to the lower sixth for the remainder of the bar. The leap between the two strands may not make a strong impression on the listener at the outset, but it represents the conflation of two voices that Haydn will later have occasion to prise apart. In the second half of the theme, the accompanying cello line descends a full octave; but the lower limit of the viola causes a kink in its descent, at *(b)*; again, the listener may make little of the difference between the two parts, even if the performers follow Haydn's subtly discrepant slurring.[3]

In the development, Haydn emphasizes the harmonic slippage towards the flat side by ensuring that the descents in all the accompanying voices of (2) are smooth octaves. This requires him to raise them above the threshold of the lowest open string and to distribute them in such a way as to convey a sense of development, for instance, by using the viola antiphonally with the cello and changing the register of the cello.

Example 9.4 Op. 20, No. 1, i, bars 1–4

The smoothness of these descents enables Haydn to introduce a harmonic procedure that, so far as I am aware, has not been used before: the stretching out of a modulatory sequence by different forms of the minor scale (Example 9.5). In bar 46, the cello plays the descending F melodic minor scale, with e♮^{1} and d♮^{1}; this is followed by the harmonic minor in the second violin (e♮^{1}–d♭^{1} in bar 47) and finally the natural minor in the second violin and viola (e♭^{1}–d♭^{1} in bar 48). In this way, Haydn can show the full range of tonal subtlety in the relatively simple modulations from E♭ through A♭ to F minor. The gradual progress towards the "correct" form can be heard clearly, because all three instruments play their scales in the same register.

Example 9.5 Op. 20, No. 1, i, bars 46–49

The next seven bars present the central harmonic progression in the development, driven by broken chords in sixteenth notes concluding with a run-out in C minor. This sort of passage is familiar in Haydn's instrumental music; we encounter similar progressions elsewhere in Op. 20 and Op. 33 as well as in the keyboard sonatas from the intervening decade. Although one can identify a source for the sixteenth-note pattern—the violin solo across bars 25–26, in the detached articulation of the cello at bars 29–30—it is difficult to avoid the feeling that the texture has been fractured: in a rerun of the battle between cello and first violin in the C major quartet, the parts are not behaving in accordance with the quartet's liberal rules of conversation. However, the passage here is much shorter and, as with the C major quartet, the brute force of the individual instruments throws into relief the more refined trio sonata textures and antiphonal pairings on either side of it.

The final phase of the development returns to the opening theme, but now emphasizes its first bar. As the motivic components of themes are naturally teased apart in a development, it is appropriate for Haydn to distribute the original upper-voice duet among three instruments (Example 9.6). In this way he is not only able to clarify the original viola part as a conflation of two voices (shown earlier in Example 9.4), but can also make effective use of all four instruments in the ensemble. In this passage, we see that he has overstepped his harmonic goal: the opening theme returns in A♭, the subdominant of the home key. But there is a twist here, too, since the theme is harmonized not with an A♭ chord but with a V–I *progression* in A♭. That is, the process of harmonic development continues despite the "arrival" of the main theme in the first violin: at *(a)* the start of the theme is harmonized by V of A♭; at *(b)* the viola's leading note resolves, but the cello's insistence on E♭ makes for a $^6_4$ chord. Finally, the cello resolves at *(c)*, setting up A♭ as a pivotal harmony for the return to the home key.

Example 9.6 Op. 20, No. 1, i, bars 64–67

In the recapitulation, the main themes return in the order in which they occurred in the exposition. One feature was to become characteristic of Haydn's recapitulations: a further, sequential development of the main theme following its return in the home key (Example 9.7). This interpolation, which is usually based on a sequential pattern, lends weight to a section deprived of a modulation to the dominant, and thus helps the larger balance between the exposition and the recapitulation. In this movement, the four-part texture contrasts effectively with the original unison version of the motive on which it is based.

Example 9.7 Op. 20, No. 1, i, bars 78–81

No other new textures are introduced, but the duets of the second theme now follow the natural registral order of the instruments: the viola is accompanied by the cello, the first violin by the second.

MENUET: UN POCO ALLEGRETTO

The main part of the minuet offers few surprises. It is an a–b–a' form, built in four- and eight-bar phrases, and has a clear modulation to the dominant in the b section. The textures, too, are free from the ambiguities that characterize the first movement. Interest revolves around three events, one in each section: the sudden lowering of dynamics and register in bar 5, the change of mode in bar 13, and the a♮² in bar 36, which replaces an earlier a♭².

At first sight, the purpose of the lower dynamics and register in bar 5 is to assist in contrasting the antecedent and consequent phrases of the piece, which establish the home key of E♭. The two phrases are, however, different in other respects: while the antecedent consists of a vigorously accompanied violin melody with a strong dotted-rhythm motive, the consequent is based on a smooth line of quarter notes accompanied in thirds (and tenths) from below. In other words, there is an element of thematic duality here, without a change of key, which will compensate for the recycling of the main theme after the double bar.

The b-section begins with a variant of the opening theme in a reduced scoring. This sets up the dramatic entrance, in B♭ minor, of the theme in its original form. The melody of bars 13–16 is closely modeled on bars 1–4, but the accompaniment is now broader, and the total compass of the four instruments is increased. The economy of Haydn's planning is shown in the next four bars, which provide a consequent to bars 13–16; it is set in B♭ *major* and cadences in the new key, so that the two four-bar phrases together constitute a contrasting idea, a kind of "second theme" of the minuet (Example 9.8). But the differences of texture and motive also give the second of these phrases the quality of a "closing theme": the melody is now doubled at the octave by the second violin and contains elements of both the dotted-figure motive and the smooth quarter notes, which had previously been kept separate.

Example 9.8 Op. 20, No. 1, ii, bars 13–20

The extension of the reprise, to more than twice the length of the opening, helps to balance the extremes of register and texture in the first eight bars. Bar 36 is analogous to bar 13: the high $a\natural^2$ in the diminished seventh chord replaces the expected ab^2 of a dominant seventh, just as the B♭ minor chord came as a shock after four bars of preparation for B♭ major. But this diminished seventh comes at the end of a four-bar unit, not the beginning, inviting Haydn to tie the chord over to the beginning of the next bar and so create the only continuous eight-bar phrase in the minuet.

There is also a tonal connection between the B♭ minor chord and the diminished seventh. The former signals a clear change in mode, the latter subtly implies one: its gb^1 is the minor third of the home key, and is brought into the higher register for a gb^2–f^2–eb^2 descent in bar 38 prior to the cadence in the major two bars later.

The last phrase not only reinforces the home key but also recalls the one passage not yet recapitulated: the start of the b-section. The direction of the dotted figure is again reversed, and the scoring is reduced, this time to two parts. The phrase is built upon a descending sequence, and by connecting the high and low E♭s in the melody it reconciles the registral extremes introduced at the start of the minuet.

The trio section starts in the key of A♭, the subdominant. Its first part is dominated by a violin solo that improvises a route to a cadence in E♭ and seems momentarily to lose its way at the db^2 in bar 50. In the second part, three leading notes and their resolutions leave the harmony poised to resolve to F minor, but the return of the main minuet theme is puzzling: this is hardly the right place for a false reprise. A greater surprise, however, is yet to come: after reaching a half cadence in F minor after four bars, Haydn introduces a full recapitulation of the minuet in the home key of E♭.

As explained in chapter 7, this movement is one of six from the years 1769–72 whose trio cannot stand as an independent piece, and one of two whose tonal relationship to the main section is difficult to explain. The V_5^6 of F minor at the end of the trio is unstable in many respects. As a dominant seventh it demands resolution, which means that the four-bar phrase to which it belongs implies a consequent phrase. But F minor is the home key neither of the trio nor of the minuet overall, so the addition of a consequent will not be of much help: indeed, the e♮^{1} underpinning the V_5^6 is in direct conflict with both the fifth of A♭ and the keynote of E♭.

Is the lead-back to the minuet defective? Can it be—could it have been— improved upon? A smooth path from V_5^6 of F minor to the tonic of E♭ is offered in Example 9.9: the chords in brackets are not Haydn's. This recomposition is much too simplistic for ears accustomed to what Haydn actually wrote, but it might provide clues as to why Haydn's version is right. What is needed at the end of the trio is (1) a resolution of the diminished fifth between b♭^{2} and e♮^{1} inwards, to a♭^{2} and f^1, followed by (2) a dominant of E♭ that will prevent the direct succession of F minor and E♭ major chords; to support the sequential harmony, a first-inversion dominant seventh chord is preferred, resulting in the progression V_5^6/ii–ii–V_5^6–I.

Example 9.9 Op. 20, No. 1, ii, bars 62–65 followed by bars 1–4, with interpolated chords

But the crucial features of the interpolated chords in Example 9.9 are actually present in the opening phrase of the minuet: the melody climbs to a♭^{2} in bar 4, while the bass reaches f^1 early on, before descending by step to d^1. In other words, while it is perfectly true that "the bass progression e♮–e♭ is anything but stable,"[4] to have stabilized the harmony in the manner suggested above would have meant a duplication of the necessary elements in the outer parts, a♭^{2} in the melody and the movement from f^1 to d^1 in the bass. In his economy of means, Haydn triumphs once again.

AFFETTUOSO E SOSTENUTO

The movement is one of only two Haydn quartet slow movements in 3/8 time, and the only slow movement lacking a conventional tempo indicator. "Sostenuto" does, of course, occur elsewhere, and "affettuoso" is used to characterize the slow movement of another Op. 20 quartet; but nowhere else do we find the two adverbs used in conjunction with one another, or to the exclusion of "largo," "adagio," "andante" or some other such marker.

The four-part sonority throughout the movement is intensified by step motion in the inner parts and the bass, and by legato in all the parts. The originality of Haydn's texture is, most probably, what attracted Mozart to it in K. 428 or, rather, what leads us to suppose that a connection exists between the two. It may be that Haydn returned Mozart the compliment by composing a sequel in the set that immediately followed the publication of Mozart's "Haydn" quartets. In the Poco adagio from Op. 50, No. 5, composed in 1787 (the movement's subtitle, The Dream, is apocryphal), the smooth flow of eighth notes is recalled, though now in 3/4 time and as an accompaniment to a decorative first violin solo. When the solo violin itself proceeds in eighth notes, as in Example 9.10, the texture is reminiscent of the Affettuoso e sostenuto.

Example 9.10 Op. 50, No. 5, ii, bars 28–33

But what of the origins of the movement's remarkable sonority? Are there precedents for the Affettuoso e sostenuto in Haydn's earlier quartets? The answer to this question is, strictly speaking, no, since the special quality of the movement resides not in the sonority of close four-part string writing but in the *prolongation of that single texture* over a long stretch of time; that texture is broken only by three short violin solos. The key of the movement supports Haydn's intentionally uniform sound: only the two lowest notes in the quartet's cycle of open strings (C–G–D–A–E) belong to the A♭ scale, so that sonorities in this key will depend more on the interaction among the instruments than on their individual resonance. A solo violin will sparkle in the key of A or E, a cello can resonate powerfully in C or on the dominant of F. In quartet movements set in flat keys, Haydn cannot capitalize on the direct or sympathetic vibration of open strings, here his lower parts tend to be more linearly conceived: the previous E♭ slow movements are good examples (Op. 9, No. 5; Op. 17, No. 4). So, too, is his only earlier slow movement in A♭, the Adagio from Op. 17,

No. 3, where the cello makes only two leaps in the opening six-bar phrase
(Example 9.11).

Example 9.11 Op. 17, No. 3, iii, bars 1–6

There is also an affinity with the other A♭ music in Op. 20, No. 1, the trio
section of the second movement. It not only shows the same dreamy quality in its
counterpoint, but its beginning uses almost the same accompaniment (Example
9.12). We now see the trio in a new light: not only does it separate the minuet
from its reprise (i.e., its "false reprise"), it anticipates both the key and character
of the movement that follows.

Example 9.12 Op. 20, No. 1, (a) ii, bars 45–48

(b) iii, bars 1–2

The four-part harmony is broken only at the full cadences in E♭ and A♭ towards the end of the exposition and recapitulation, respectively. A third violin solo, which emerges briefly at the end of a passage of harmonic development, provides an additional form marker by preparing the return of the opening theme in the home key. The movement thus has all the ingredients of sonata form, but the lack of contrasting textures diverts the ear from events that, in a more conventional context, would sound more dramatic. The repeat marks on both sides of the central double bar, when they are observed, further incline us to perceive the movement as a binary form.

Haydn's general dynamic marking, *mezza voce*, supports the textural uniformity of the movement (only the final phrase, *piano–pianissimo* over a tonic pedal, departs from this instruction). So does his phrase structure, which favors irregular groupings, as shown in Table 9.1. Five-bar groups are almost the norm, except in the development section, where a discursive harmony is assisted by the clarity of a regular phrase structure.[5]

Table 9.1

Op. 20, No. 1, phrase structure of the Affettuoso e sostenuto

Exposition	5+2	statement of main theme
	5	move toward dominant key, E♭
	6	phrase in E♭ ending with half-cadence
	1+4	sequence, leading to inconclusive resolution in E♭
	1+4+5	repeat of sequence, continuation (with violin solo) and full E♭ cadence
	2+3	closing phrase, affirming E♭
Development	5	statement of main theme in E♭
	4+4	modulation to D♭, by way of B♭ minor
	4+4	sequential progression and continuation towards V^7 of IV (A♭^{7})
	5+3	return to A♭ by way of harmonic progression V^7/IV–IV–V
Recapitulation	5+4	statement of main theme in A♭, with phrase leading to V
	1+4	sequence, leading to inconclusively resolution in A♭
	1+4+5	repeat of sequence, continuation (with violin solo) and full A♭ cadence
	2+3	closing phrase, affirming A♭

To the density of texture and the irregularity of phrasing should be added a further complementary characteristic of this movement: the contrast between open and close harmony, that is, between widely spaced part-writing and the crossing of parts that causes momentary melodic or harmonic ambiguity. (Again, the development section is largely free of this ambiguity: the only part-crossings here are between second violin and viola.) The register of the cello is crucial for the type of chord spacing encountered and, as was shown earlier, a play between

Example 9.13 Op. 20, No. 1, iii, bars 19–34

high and low is characteristic of cello parts in slow movements in flat keys. The Affettuoso e sostenuto reverses Haydn's normal direction, from high to low: the cello aims immediately for the open C in bar 5, then pushes upward in the counterstatement of the opening theme and the modulation to the second group, until only a fifth separates it from the first violin in bars 19–26.

Of course, part-crossings that make the cello, as functional bass, a sounding inner part are a familiar feature of Haydn's counterpoint, and it has been well established that such part-crossings are found across his entire output of quartets, from the 1750s to the late 1790s.[6] In the second group (see Example 9.13), however, we find a variety of crossings, only some involving the cello. At *(a)* the viola reaches underneath the cello's bass line, at *(b)* the first-violin melody dips below an "inner" second-violin part, and at *(c)* the second violin swoops under both the viola and the cello. Many of these part-crossings can usually be "explained" as the result of avoiding parallel fifths. At *(a)* the viola cannot use the higher b♭^{1} (or a♭^{1} in the next bar); otherwise, it would become locked in a series of parallel fifths with the first violin. The same restriction governs the second violin at *(b)*. As for the crossing of a melodic line into the inner parts, or the crossing of inner parts, this is often the result of the lower registral limits, the violin G string and the viola C string. (The end of the movement provides a good example of this.) But sometimes the melodic integrity of the solo part as a whole prevents Haydn from allowing it to climb too high. At *(d)* the beginning of the violin solo is controlled by b♭^{1} and its upper neighbor, c^2 (this register is established at the start of the movement), and not by the high f^2 and $e\flat^2$ reached by leap in bars 20–22. In the consequent phrase, the higher register is brought into play, as the resolution of $e\flat^2$ to d^2 (e) and of d^2 to $e\flat^2$ (f) over unstable harmonies delays the definitive resolution of the melody at the lower octave (g).[7]

FINALE: PRESTO

The finale serves as a reminder that Op. 20 is not an isolated achievement in Haydn's quartet oeuvre, but rather the culmination of about four years of intensive engagement with the genre. Avoiding both the academic rigor of the fugue and the modernity of the gypsy style, it reverts to the category of lighthearted binary movement in which an almost trivial main theme couples the violins in thirds. In this Presto, Haydn builds a three-bar phrase around a descending scale figure, from which he is able to derive the second theme by inverting the direction of the scale and changing its articulation. By using a closing theme that is similarly based on scale-like figures in parallel thirds, he creates a seamless effect at the main junctures of the movement, namely, the repeat of the first half, the start of the second half, and the repeat of the second half.[8] The use of scales in parallel thirds makes the Presto of Op. 17, No. 1, in E major a close relation—the first theme of the earlier quartet becomes, in effect, the second theme of the later one—but the finales of Op. 9, No. 3, and Op. 17 Nos. 2, 5, and 6, are also cousins.

While thematic connections with earlier movements show a unifying role (these are considered in chapter 10), the Presto has a forward-pressing rhythmic vitality not evident earlier in the quartet. By establishing an antecedent-consequent phrase structure based on an irregular three-bar grouping, Haydn stores up potential energy in his themes, which he is then able to unleash by switching to a regular phrase structure, for instance, at bar 11 and, with even greater force, at the beginning of the development (Example 9.14). Note in particular the "kick" at bar 60, where the three-bar grouping is suddenly abandoned.

Example 9.14 Op. 20, No. 1, iv, bars 56–63

Syncopation plays an important role in the three harmonically unstable passages: the transition to the second group, the development section, and the recapitulation of the transition. Haydn increases the tension generated here by opposing two forms of syncopation in opposition to one another. In one form (see *(a)* in Example 9.15), the melodic line is smooth and the last eighth note of one bar is tied over to the first eighth of the next, while the accompaniment proceeds in a steady quarter-note pulse. In the other, marked *(b)*, the melodic line is jagged and the two eighth notes that straddle the bar line, though still at the same pitch, are articulated separately; a rest on the downbeat in the accompaniment adds to the rhythmic instability. The three passages featuring syncopation have a ternary design, with the more disruptive syncopations with jagged lines occupying a central position, the gentler form acting as links with the other sections of the movement.[9] In the development section, syncopated figures account for more than half the music. Here the join between the jagged and smooth forms becomes more dynamic, with the second violin's octave descent (bar 79) preparing the change of articulation in the top part.

Example 9.15 Op. 20, No. 1, iv, bars 78–81

The dynamic marking in bar 79 is the first *fortissimo* in a Haydn quartet that applies to an extended passage. It marks the start of 21 bars of the jagged form of the syncopation, in which the daring crossing of an enharmonic divide is signalled by a sudden *piano* and a special slur, instructing the viola not to change the pitch when C♯ is respelled as D♭ (Example 9.16).[10]

Example 9.16 Op. 20, No. 1, iv, bars 88–94

The length and vigor of the development section—the retransition to the home key is marked by a return to *forte*—leads Haydn, unprecedentedly, to recapitulate the opening theme *piano*, and thus to allow the inversion of texture six bars later to be supported by a change of dynamics (Example 9.17).

Example 9.17 Op. 20, No.1, iv, (a) bars 105–9

(b) Bars 113–16

In all other respects, the recapitulation follows the exposition. Only at the very end does Haydn stretch out the final cadence with a chord rich in appoggiaturas, perhaps to strengthen its link with the close of the first movement (Example 9.18).[11]

Example 9.18 Op. 20, No. 1, (a) i, bar 105–6b

(b) iv, bars 156–60

10

Epilogue

The foregoing study has attempted to identify crucial features of mid-eighteenth-century string quartet style and see how they inform the composition of a set of large-scale works by the first master of the genre. My focus on details has meant some sacrifice in the discussion of the larger picture, for instance, interrelationships between movements in a work and between works in a set. For the quartets of Haydn's Op. 9 and Op. 17 in particular, the unifying and common features have yet to be assessed. The matter of unity within and between eighteenth-century string quartets must, however, be approached with caution.

INTERRELATIONSHIPS BETWEEN MOVEMENTS

In my discussion of the individual quartets of Op. 20, I noted a few thematic connections between movements. These are among the easier kinds of analytical observations, and they do not constitute the primary source of the depth and integrity that we sense in much Classical chamber music. Moreover, a handful of thematic resemblances in unexpected places cannot lead to a "cyclic" view of a work: the less consistently thematic connections are forged, the more careful we should be about conferring a primary structuring role upon those that do come to light. The concept of thematic transformation, well established for certain nineteenth-century composers such as Schumann, Liszt, and Brahms, has limited application in the music up to the time of Beethoven. Tovey's well-known critique of the thematic process, that it is neither a guarantee nor even a principal ingredient of "logical coherence,"[1] may be something of an overstatement for the Romantics but is generally accepted by writers on the Classical period.

A second danger of viewing the eighteenth-century string quartet as traversing a single dynamic curve from the opening bars of its first movement to the final cadence of the last has to do with our expectations of its finale. Coming as it does at the end, it is all too easy for us to expect this movement to fulfill a culminating function, as it does, say, in such works by Beethoven as the Fifth and Ninth Symphonies and the C♯ minor quartet. With regard to Haydn's Op. 20, it is a mistake not only to construe the fugal finale as engineering a shift from an old to a new style of counterpoint, but also to make it bear the responsibility for resolving tensions between old and new styles in earlier movements. In attending a performance of a complex work, we are bound to remember what we have heard last, and Haydn's combination of *galant* and learned styles in his final fugues is handled with such skill that we might easily be swept away by it, forgetting the subtleties of earlier movements. Our greater familiarity with Beethoven's "Hammerklavier" Sonata and the Quartet in B♭, Op. 130, with its original fugal finale, and with Mozart's "Jupiter" Symphony, may encourage us to listen to the three Op. 20 quartet fugues with anachronistic hindsight, as precursors to a later tradition in which a closing fugue indeed marks the culmination of a work of larger proportions. Whatever one reads into the early fugues, Haydn made no further contributions along these lines, at least not in his chamber music: the fugal textures in his later quartets are seamlessly woven into the fabric of sonata or variation movements. His only other quartet finale cast as a fugue, Op. 50, No. 4, is not only shorter than any of the Op. 20 fugal finales, but is also by far the shortest finale of the set to which it belongs.[2]

One may argue that these two purportedly unifying features, fugal finality and thematic interrelation, produce striking results when harnessed together in Op. 20. The semitonal symmetries between F–E♮ and C–D♭ in the principal subject of the F minor fugue, for instance, appear as early as the first two bars of the quartet's opening Allegro moderato. Yet these intervals are characteristic features of the F minor scale, and are likely to be exploited in any thematic material presented in this key. That the head-motive of Haydn's fugue subject is a characteristic Baroque figure is further grounds for being cautious about making thematic relationships mean too much.

The other two works with closing fugues are in major keys, and thematic connections between the outer movements are difficult to locate. The first movement of the A major quartet has never been linked thematically with the finale; as shown in chapter 5, similarities of rhythm, contour, and texture mark the first movement and the Menuet much more readily as cousins.[3] The fugue subject of the third fugal quartet, in C major, shows no evidence whatever of thematic kinship with the opening Moderato; in fact it may serve as a counterexample, since its nearest thematic relative in Op. 20 is found in the second group of the opening Allegro di molto e scherzando from No. 6 in A major, with which it shares a 6/8 meter:

[Allegro di molto e scherzando]

Example 10.1 (a) Op. 20, No. 6, i, bars 42–44, first violin

Allegro
sempre sotto voce

(b) Op. 20, No. 2, iv, bars 1–4, first violin

COMPLEMENTARITY

In what order did Haydn write these quartets, and how is the opus best considered as group of works rather than six individual works? These are questions that have received general attention elsewhere, and the results need only be summarized here.[4]

There has been much argument about the correct ordering of the Op. 20 quartets. The numerical ordering set down in Haydn's catalogue of his works (followed in this book) places them in two subgroups of three, those with fugues preceding those with sonata-form finales. The six autograph scores, each of which is bound separately, offer few clues to the order of composition, but if Haydn's naming of the lowest part is more than haphazard, then the quartets may well have been composed in different order.

In the manuscript sources for the earliest quartets, the lowest part is designated "Basso" even when a cello was undoubtedly required, as in Op. 9. In the Op. 17 autographs Haydn wrote "Basso," then added a clarifying "Violoncello" beneath. For Op. 20, László Somfai has shown that the definitive change of terminology from "Basso" to "Violoncello" coincides with a shift in position of the minuet from before the slow movement to after it, which may be a sign of more modern quartet planning.

Table 10.1, based on Somfai's research,[5] shows the transition during the writing of quartet autographs. It is dangerous to draw conclusions about com-positional priority from this evidence, since Haydn did much of his composing at the keyboard and wrote out his music only at a relatively late stage. It may be that the order in which the Op. 20 quartets were copied out follows Table 10.1, how-ever unlikely it seems for the strangest piece in the set—the G minor quartet—to be the first he composed.

In each of Haydn's sets from Op. 9 to Op. 76, the quartets are written in differ-ent keys, one of these being a minor key. Variety is sometimes enhanced by making one of the first movements livelier or in some way more "violinistic" than the others, for instance by being set in a faster tempo (Presto or Allegro di

Table 10.1

Naming of the lowest part in the Op. 20 autograph scores

No. 3 in G minor	"Basso"
No. 1 in E♭ and No. 5 in F minor	"Basso" changed to "Violoncello"
No. 2 in C and No. 6 in A	"Violoncello"
No. 4 in D	(no marking)

molto), a bright key (e.g. A major), or a time signature of 6/8, or a combination of these. Half of his sets of quartets include a work that opens with a theme and variations, and in the remaining sets, variations figure prominently as slow movements or finales.

As a set, opus 20 is remarkable mainly for its concentration of fugal finales. The variety of forms and styles in the other movements is about the same as we find elsewhere. The absence of an opening variation set is compensated for by the Un poco adagio e affettuoso of No. 4, the first variation set for string quartet to be extended by a substantial coda. It is noteworthy that two, not one, of the six works are in minor keys and that of the four in major, two have substantial and striking slow movements set in the tonic minor. Do these factors—fugue, and the greater proportion of movements in minor keys—invite us to conclude that Op. 20 is a more "serious" set of works? I think not; but because they have become *better known* than works like Op. 9, No. 4, in D minor, or Op. 17, No. 4, in C minor, or the dramatic slow movements of Op. 9, No. 2, and Op. 17, No. 5, it is easy for us to make a one-directional comparison, between Op. 20 and what followed.

FINAL THOUGHTS

Historians have singled out Op. 33 as marking the start of Haydn's quartet writing with a lighter touch. Were we to judge the two sets on the basis of first movements, though, I believe that Op. 20 could be seen as equally modern in its outlook and that, despite the chronology and ignoring the handful of movements in both sets that recall earlier works (the finale of Op. 20, No. 1, and the slow movement of Op. 33, No. 5, would probably feel more at home in Op. 9 or Op. 17), the difference between Op. 20 and its immediate predecessors is in some respects more profound than that between it and its much later successors:

It is true that the individual movements in Op. 20 are longer and that their themes are developed at greater length than we find in Op. 33. Compared to Op. 9 and Op. 17, the cello also has a much bigger role to play in thematic presentation and development (though its prominence does not come as a complete surprise), and this is a feature that Haydn set aside while composing the next set.[6]

Haydn advertised his Op. 33 as composed "in a new and entirely special way." But we can turn the clause that follows (and supports) this claim, "for I haven't written any quartets in 10 years," on its head and read the development of the string quartet in a different way. Unlike Op. 33, which came after a long break, Op. 20 resulted from an intense affair with the quartet, and marks the culmination of concentrated thinking about the problems in part-writing and ensemble technique. It was the three-year period from 1769 to 1772, not the nine-year gap that followed, that resulted in a set of quartets of hitherto unknown richness and depth of feeling.

The main purpose of my discussion of individual quartets in chapters 4 to 9 was to exemplify the application of quartet composition techniques to whole pieces, that is, the successful alliance of four-part solo string writing with sonata forms and their associated styles. I hope that the principles I have developed here will also be useful elsewhere and that, making allowances for changes in musical style and organization, they can also be applied to later string chamber music of the Classical period. While much has been written about this repertory, the relationship of texture to design merits closer attention. If the present study stimulates further work in this field, it will have fulfilled its primary goal.

Notes

Chapter 1: Introduction

1. In his *Studien zur Geschichte des Streichquartetts, I: Die Enstehung des klassichen Streichquartetts, von den Vorformen zur Grundlegung durch Joseph Haydn* (Kassel: Bärenreiter, 1974), Ludwig Finscher dubbed these works "quartet-divertimenti"; see, especially the section "Quadro und Quartettdivertimento," pp. 84–105. The term found favor with Robbins Landon, who adopted it in his discussion of the early quartets in the first volume of his *Haydn: Chronicle and Works* (London: Thames and Hudson, 1980), p. 254. Dean Sutcliffe has observed that "divertimento" appears in authentic sources as the title of Haydn quartets up to 1781, but still finds the term "quartet-divertimento" "very fitting" for Opp. 1–2, owing to the presence of two minuets in a five-movement form in all ten works; see his *Haydn: String Quartets, Op. 50* (Cambridge: Cambridge University Press, 1992), p. 2. James Webster has stressed that, in its original usage, the word "divertimento" had none of the connotations of lightness that it was to acquire by the late eighteenth century; see his article "Towards a History of Viennese Chamber Music in the Early Classical Period," *Journal of the American Musicological Society* 27 (1974), pp. 212–47, especially pp. 215–21.

2. See, for example, Georg Feder's list of works for the "Haydn" entry in *The New Grove Dictionary of Music and Musicians*, ed. Stanley Sadie (London: Macmillan, 1980), vol. 8, pp. 378–79. For a more comprehensive study, see James Webster, "The Chronology of Haydn's String Quartets," *Musical Quarterly* 61 (1975), pp. 17–46.

3. Landon, *Haydn: Chronicle and Works*, vol. 2 (London: Thames and Hudson, 1978), p. 317.

4. Hans Keller, *The Great Haydn Quartets: Their Interpretation* (London: Dent, 1986).

5. An exception is James Webster's highly original though necessarily brief study of form in the quartets of Opp. 1–2, fittingly published as the final paper in the proceedings

of the International Haydn Conference held in Washington, D.C., in 1975: "Freedom of Form in Haydn's Early String Quartets," in *Haydn Studies*, ed. Jens Peter Larsen, Howard Serwer, and James Webster (New York: Norton, 1980), pp. 522–30. There are also several finely judged accounts of form in the early quartets in the revised edition of Charles Rosen's *Sonata Forms* (New York: Norton, 1988), compensating for the neglect of these works in his earlier book, *The Classical Style* (London: Faber and Faber, 1971).

6. "Das Streichquartett ist die verständlichste aller Instrumentalgattungen. Man hört vier vernünftige Leute sich miteinander unterhalten, glaubt ihren Diskursen etwas abzugewinnen und die Eigentümlichkeiten der Instrumente kennenzulernen." Quoted in Heinrich Eduard Jacob, *Joseph Haydn: seine Kunst, seine Zeit, sein Ruhm* (Hamburg: Wegener, 1954), p. 134 (my translation). The context for this remark is often overlooked: it comes from a letter to Carl Friedrich Zelter, director of the Singakademie in Berlin, in which the writer expresses his disappointment at a concert given by Paganini.

7. "Als er das B Quartett beendigt hatte, sagte ich, daß ich es doch für das größte von den dreien (Op. 127, 130, 132) halte. Er antwortete: *jedes in seiner Art!* Die Kunst will es von uns, daß wir, so sprach er häufig scherzhaft im Kaiserstyl, nicht stehen bleiben. Sie werden eine neue Art der Stimmführung bemerken (hiemit ist die Instrumentirung, die Vertheilung der Rollen gemeint) und *an Fantasie fehlt's, Gottlob, weniger als je zuvor.*" The anecdote is transmitted in Wilhelm von Lenz, *Beethoven, eine Kunststudie*, vol. 5 (Hamburg: Hoffmann und Campe, 1860), p. 217 (my translation).

8. In Georg August Griesinger's *Biographische Notizen über Joseph Haydn* (1810). See Vernon Gotwals, ed. and trans., *Haydn: Two Contemporary Portraits* (Madison: University of Wisconsin Press 1968), p. 13.

Chapter 2: Anatomy of the Quartet

1. "Die unnatürliche Wuth, die man hat, sogar *Klaviersachen* auf Geigeninstrumente überzupflanzen, Instrumente, die so einander in allem entgegengesetzt sind . . . da nicht allein ganze Stellen gänzlich wegbleiben und umgeändert werden müssen, so muß man—noch hinzutun," letter to Breitkopf und Härtel in Leipzig, 13 July 1802. See *Ludwig van Beethoven: Briefwechsel Gesamtausgabe*, Sieghard Brandenburg, ed., vol. 1 (Munich: Henle, 1996), letter 92. To be sure, there is a touch of insincerity on Beethoven's part if his arrangement of Op. 14, No. 1, is to serve as a guide: it adheres to its original more faithfully than Haydn's in all respects except that of key (being transposed to the more quartet-friendly F major). Most of the changes of motive and part-writing occur in the finale, but nowhere have bars been inserted or omitted, as the letter might suggest.

2. For an example, see Finscher, *Geschichte des Streichquartetts*, p. 51.

3. Neither marking, *con sordino* or "Echo," appears in the Eulenburg miniature score.

4. Haydn revived the echo technique in a later chamber work. In the opening Andantino of Trio No. 107 in D major, for violin, viola and baryton (ca. 1772) the viola is marked *con sordino* and responds similarly to the ends of the violin phrases.

5. Donald F. Tovey, "Haydn, Franz Joseph," in *Cobbett's Cyclopedic Survey of Chamber Music*, W. W. Cobbett, ed. (London: Oxford University Press, 1929), vol. 1, p. 522.

6. In the second recitative passage, the appoggiaturas are notated either as grace notes or fully written-out eighth notes; in the earlier passage in the movement, some appoggiaturas are given as grace-note quarters. It is unclear whether these notations mean different things (the quarter-notes may specify a longer appoggiatura), or whether Haydn is inconsistently switching between a notation for singers and one for instrumentalists who would not be familiar with the conventions of applying appoggiaturas to dramatic music. Nonetheless, the rhythmic freedom needed to make the movement effective—most of the recitative will sound too slow at the prescribed *adagio*—is left for the players to work out for themselves.

7. There is a certain irony in the fact that this Baroque aria, as it has been described, belongs to the quartet that opens a set of works described by their composer as having been written "in an entirely new and special way." For insight into this movement, and especially the final *pizzicato*, see Sutcliffe, *Haydn: String Quartets, Op. 50*, p. 23.

8. The siciliano in Haydn's next quartet opus seems, in contrast to Op. 9, No. 1, to be a simpler affair. Despite interaction between the parts in certain passages (bars 4–8 and 31–32 in the exposition) there are long stretches in the third movement of Op. 17, No. 1, in which aria mode prevails, with the lower strings providing a backdrop of accompaniment for the solo violin.

9. For the application of *messa di voce* to eighteenth-century instrumental technique, see Johann Joachim Quantz's *Versuch einer Anweisung, die Flöte traversiere zu spielen* (1752), section xiv, paragraph 10. Leopold Mozart does not mention this technique by name in his *Gründliche Violinschule* of 1756, but describes the wonderful effect produced when a long note in an *adagio* is decorated by changes in dynamics (chapter 5, paragraph 4); throughout the chapter on tone production, Mozart stresses the singing quality of expressive violin playing.

10. In a rich and varied discussion of textural "signs" in Classical music, Janet Levy argues that "probably the single most pervasive quality of a unison passage is its aura of authoritative control," which, she claims, "is basically contrary to our sense of the individuality of human beings"; see her "Texture as a Sign in Classic and Early Romantic Music," *Journal of the American Musicological Society* 35 (1982), p. 507. Levy does not remark on the distinct effects of unisons in different textures, for instance, the symphony and the string quartet, and, as I have argued earlier, a unison in a string quartet may often convey the impression of a symphony. Her idea that the unison represents loss of identity nonetheless rings true. When the quartet plays in unison, conversation ceases: the instruments lose their individuality, which was their main purpose for convening.

11. The best studies of this problem are a pair of articles by James Webster, "Violoncello and Double Bass in the Chamber Music of Haydn and His Viennese Contemporaries, 1750–1780," *Journal of the American Musicological Society* 29 (1976), pp. 413–438; and "The Bass Part in Haydn's Early String Quartets," *Musical Quarterly* 63 (1977), pp. 390–424. The "problem" of the cello part in Haydn's quartets, namely, that it is sometimes notated above the viola while still continuing to function as a bass, has been explored in considerable depth by Webster and will not be elaborated on here. It will suffice to repeat Webster's main conclusions, namely that (1) these part-crossings, which occur regularly in Haydn's oeuvre from the 1750s to the 1790s, offer in themselves no

evidence that the lowest part of his early quartets should be taken by a double bass, and (2) the harmonic infelicities that they engender, especially root-position triads sounding as $^6_4$ chords, feature in a transitional phase of chamber music composition in which the cello was "liberated" from its role as a bass and began to take on a more soloistic role in the ensemble. For further thoughts on composers of a transitional phase, see my study "The Cello Part in Beethoven's Late Quartets," *Beethoven Forum* 7 (1999), p. 58, note 10.

12. The slow movement Op. 33, No. 2, has as its main theme an eight-bar duet conceived along the lines of the opening period from the theme of Op. 50, No. 3, and it is also cast in B♭. I am tempted to suggest that it was originally conceived as a cello solo. The viola could easily have taken the bass up to the cadence in bar 8, at which point its lower limit (the open c) proved one note too high for the required tonic; Haydn was therefore obliged to rewrite the theme as a viola solo. He solved the problem in Op. 50, No. 3, by making the cello revert to the bass for the final two notes of the eighth bar.

13. This passage has been cited by Webster ("The Bass Part in Haydn's Early String Quartets," p. 399) as evidence supporting performance of the lowest part of Haydn's earliest quartets on the cello.

14. Pierre Baillot's celebrated *L'art du violon* (Paris: Imprimerie du Conservatoire de Musique, 1834), for example, includes extracts from Haydn first violin parts from Op. 9 to Op. 76 as well as extracts from various chamber works by Mozart and Beethoven. For illustrations of these, see Robin Stowell, *Violin Technique and Performance Practice in the Late Eighteenth and Early Nineteenth Centuries* (Cambridge: Cambridge University Press, 1983), *passim*.

15. The part-writing in bar 26 would be improved if the bass were written an octave lower, i.e. taken by the viola.

16. For the finale of Op. 33, No. 4, the metaphor of evaporation seems especially appropriate: the *pizzicato* slows down the first violin, preventing it from producing all the notes of the original theme.

17. See, for instance, Leopold Mozart's injunction against open strings in his *Gründliche Violinschule*, chapter 5, paragraph 13.

18. It is striking that each of the nine sets of six quartets by Haydn, from Op. 9 to Op. 76, contains one work in the key of C; the keys of D and G are represented in all but one opus, whereas F appears only five times (and once more in Op. 77). By contrast, Beethoven showed a clear preference for F, the key in which he set four of his sixteen quartets plus the arrangement of Op. 14, No. 1 (transposed from E major); he wrote only two quartets in C, and one each in G and D. In Haydn, then, the open strings tend to enhance the volume of sound; in Beethoven, by contrast, their function is more often "strategic," that is, as the dominant of F.

Of course, generalizations are not of much help when explaining the use of open strings in individual cases. As has been noted earlier, one of the strongest bits of evidence for assigning the bass part to the cello in Opp. 1–2 is that in the slow movement of Op. 2, No. 4, the open C is used strategically, as the dominant of F minor, with intensification from a D♭ neighbor.

For further details on open strings in the Classical quartet, see my studies "Beethoven and the Open String," *Music Analysis* 4 (1985), pp. 15–28; "Fingering in Haydn's

Quartets," *Early Music* 16 (1988), pp. 50–57; and "The Cello Part in Beethoven's Late Quartets," especially pp. 62–65.

19. Hans Keller has argued that mutes have no place in the performance of great string chamber music, that they produce "an invalid quartet sound" (*The Great Haydn Quartets*, p. 9). To be sure, Keller made this point as part of a general dismissal of the Op. 3 set, now believed not to be by Haydn, which contains the once-famous "Serenade" that is scored in the same way as the Adagio of Op. 1, No. 6: muted first violin plus *pizzicato* lower strings. He was also well aware of the use of mutes in the slow movement of Mozart's G minor quintet, and included a plausible explanation for this.

20. Of course, a quartet can begin immediately as a dialogue, as if the instruments had been introduced to one another beforehand, so to speak. See Charles Rosen's excellent analysis of the "conversation" that initiates Haydn's Op. 54, No. 3, in *The Classical Style*, pp. 141–42.

21. For a comprehensive discussion of the various orderings of the quartets, including speculation about their relative chronology, see Landon, *Haydn: Chronicle and Works*, vol. 2, pp. 325–27.

Chapter 3: Fugue

1. Ludwig Finscher's idea that the fugues fail to behave convincingly as finales to these quartets (*Geschichte des Streichquartetts*, p. 235) is typical of the negative judgements. For a summary and critique of Op. 20's principal detractors—Adolf Sandberger, Friedrich Blume, and Finscher—see the section "Sandberger's Tale" in Webster's *Haydn's "Farewell" Symphony and the Idea of Classical Style* (Cambridge: Cambridge University Press, 1991), pp. 341–47.

2. Early examples of string quartet movements in fugal texture include pieces by Frantisek Xaver Richter (1709–89) and Carlo d'Ordonez (1734–86); see note 13 later in this section. Haydn's interest in the fugal finale in the early 1770s extends to the trio for baryton, viola, and bass, a genre he cultivated at the behest of his employer, Prince Nicholas Esterhazy. Three of these pieces (nos. 97, 101, and 114) end with fugues. For a fuller background, see Warren Kirkendale, *Fugue and Fugato in Rococo and Classical Chamber Music.* (Durham, NC: Duke University Press, 1979).

3. Kirkendale, *Fugue and Fugato*, p. 144. Kirkendale attributes this judgement in part to the extraordinarily large number of entries, yet most of these are truncations of the subject to its five-note head-motive.

4. Webster, *Haydn's "Farewell" Symphony*, p. 295.

5. Finscher, *Geschichte des Streichquartetts*, p. 232.

6. The case of K. 387, the first of Mozart's quartets of the 1780s, is instructive: neither the multiple subjects in the second group (bars 69ff., 209ff.) nor the techniques of *stretto* and canon in the coda (bars 282ff.) make the finale sound especially learned.

7. Kirkendale, *Fugue and Fugato*, p. 142.

8. This symmetry, which is later exploited in the long canon between the first violin and the cello (bars 145–57), is one reason why Haydn may have "modified" the intervallic structure of the subject, which has sometimes been compared unfavorably with the

version in the *Messiah* chorus. Handel makes the second note a♭¹, rather than f¹; had Haydn used the earier form of the subject, his canon would have been less effective.

9. After the opening exposition, which comprises five entries of the subject, a transition leads to the relative key of A major. The arrival in the new key is marked by four entries of the theme, in A, E, A, and D (I–V–I–IV reckoned in terms of A); the greater number of entries compensates for the brevity of the subject. At this point the harmony becomes more discursive, and fragments of the main theme appear increasingly in the counterpoint. For the "recapitulation," which arrives halfway through the movement, Haydn treats the subject in *stretto*, with entries every bar on F♯, C♯, C♯, and F♯ (i.e. i–v–v–i reckoned in the home key), but the texture from this point onwards is mainly homophonic.

The underpinning of the Op. 50, No. 4, fugue by sonata form was the subject of a paper presented by Sharon Choa at the Conference on Music Analysis held at the University of Cambridge in July 1997.

10. Sutcliffe, *Haydn: String Quartets, Op. 50*, p. 90.

11. For a different reading of this opening statement, see Webster, *Haydn's "Farewell" Symphony*, p. 295.

12. The finale of No. 6, which maintains its strict contrapuntal stance for longer than any other Haydn quartet fugue, reverses the trajectory of the quartet as a whole from the witty (fast opening movement in a bright key in 6/8 time) to the serious (strict fugue in common time). No satisfactory explanation for this has been proposed, other than the usual opt-out clause in Haydn criticism, namely, that his forms are unpredictable: he never quite does the same thing twice.

13. The finale of the B♭ quartet from Richter's first set of quartets, published in 1768, is a "Fugato" in binary form and combines fugal and homophonic textures. In this respect it anticipates Mozart's Quartet in G, K. 387 much more than does Haydn's Op. 20, though it lacks both Mozart's combinatorial thematic ingenuity and his imaginative sonata design. A modern edition of this quartet, based on a manuscript source, was published in Frantisek Xaver Richter, *Divertimenti per quartetto d'archi*, Musica Antiqua Bohemica 71 (Prague: Editio Supraphon, 1969).

Four of the six quartets of Carlo d'Ordonez's Op. 1, first published in 1777, also include movements that are substantially based on fugal construction. According to Peter Brown, who prepared a modern edition of the score (Carlo d'Ordonez, *String Quartets, Opus 1,* Madison: AR Editions, 1980), the quartets were "probably composed in the 1760s," that is, before Haydn's Op. 20, though no evidence is offered in support of this claim.

According to Kirkendale (*Fugue and Fugato*, p. 279), the works of Haydn's teacher, Gregor Werner (1693–1766), include a manuscript set of six fugues for two violins, viola and bass ("Fondament").

Chapter 4: Quartet in F Minor, Op. 20, No. 5

1. Rosen, *The Classical Style*, p. 118.

2. The dynamic markings in the traditional editions, which call for a gradual decrescendo from *ff* to *pp* across these two harmonic cycles, are corrupt.

3. This passage is sometimes seen as a forerunner to the rhapsodic slow movement from the Quartet in C, Op. 54, No. 2, which likewise features a highly ornamented first violin part above a chordal accompaniment. In the later work, however, the solo part is rhythmically irregular throughout, and it would be more accurate to describe its implied harmony as moving in and out of phase with the accompaniment rather than being metrically "retarded." Another piece worth comparing is the Rondo of Mozart's oboe quartet in F, K. 370, composed nine years after Haydn's Op. 20, which includes a virtuoso passage *alla breve* for the oboe (sixteen sixteenth notes per bar) against a jaunty 6/8 string accompaniment (Example 4. 13). Although there is no displacement of harmony between solo and accompaniment, stratification between solo wind and strings is achieved by the opposition of meter and style.

Example 4. 13 Mozart, Quartet in F for Oboe and Strings, K. 370, No. iii, bars 103–8

Not only are the key and meter of the two movements the same, the passages in question are comparable in length and follow the same basic harmonic progression. They also function in the same way: to prepare a recapitulation of the main theme. Of course, Haydn's thirty-second notes are expressive rather than virtuoso, but that is a difference one would expect between an Adagio and a final Allegro.

4. In *The Great Haydn Quartets*, Hans Keller implies that a siciliano must be a somewhat lively dance and that the Allegretto of Op. 33, No. 5, is a true siciliano whereas the Adagio of Op. 20, No. 5, is not. This does not seem to be borne out either by contemporary writings, which call the siciliano a "slow gigue," or by tempo markings used by other eighteenth-century composers for works cast in a lilting 6/8 or 12/8. Though *allegretto* occurs frequently, there are also famous examples marked *larghetto, andante* and

andantino. Haydn's quartet siciliano movements are marked *adagio* as often as they are marked *allegretto*.

Chapter 5: Quartet in A Major, Op. 20, No. 6

1. Tovey, "Haydn, Franz Joseph," p. 537; Tovey, *Musical Articles from the Encyclopaedia Britannica* (London: Oxford University Press, 1944), pp. 217–19; Tovey, *Beethoven*, ed. Hubert J. Foss (London: Oxford University Press, 1944), pp. 41–42.

2. Tovey, *Musical Articles from the Encyclopaedia Britannica*, pp. 217–18.

3. Haydn originally wrote bar 102 with an extra dotted quarter's worth of rest between the last two notes, in effect as a 9/8 bar. He may have omitted the rest to avoid blurring the effect of the longer caesura before the start of the recapitulation, or he may have thought that a 9/8 bar might risk creating confusion about the new metric position of the closing subject.

4. Ternary and binary designs are similarly combined in the slow movements of Op. 9, No. 2, and Op. 17, No. 4, whose forms closely resemble that of the Adagio of Op. 20, No. 6. In each of the other two slow movements with varied repeats of their expositions, Op. 9, No. 4, and Op. 33, No. 3, the b-section includes a return of the main theme as we would find in sonata form, that is, a further written-out embellishment of the theme in the home key. For Haydn to revert to a simpler melodic design would have been strategically inappropriate, as sonata movements with varied reprises are hybrids of sonata and variation forms and demand "through-composed" planning.

Chapter 6: Quartet in C Major, Op. 20, No. 2

1. The quiet growth of the second-violin motive from two notes (c^2–b^1) to four (e^2–d^2–c^2–b^1), finds its culmination when the new theme in the first violin brings the imitation f^2–e^2–d^2–c^2. The entire process is devalued by the corrupt text of the Eulenburg score, in which the notes in bar 70 are wrong and the dynamics are either missing (bars 65–66) or incorrect (bars 71–74).

2. The critic who wrote most consistently on this matter in the English language was Donald Tovey; see, for example, "Normality and Freedom in Music" and especially "Some Aspects of Beethoven's Art-Forms" (both in his *Essays and Lectures on Music*, ed. Hubert Foss [London: Oxford University Press, 1949]). For an alternative point of view, which discusses Beethoven's concept of form as comprising a number of fixed elements, see my essay "Beethoven's Understanding of 'Sonata Form': The Evidence of the Sketchbooks," in *Beethoven's Compositional Process*, ed. W. Kinderman (Lincoln: University of Nebraska Press, 1991), pp. 14–19.

3. The Adagio of Op. 76, No. 6, in B major, subtitled Fantasia, exhibits an altogether different kind of freedom. To the extent that the main theme and a modulatory episode alternate with one another for most of the duration of the piece, the form is regular, but the modulations take in so many different keys in the first sixty bars—the main theme alone returns in E, B♭, and A♭—that it would be inappropriate to speak of a rondo, or even a theme and variations. Haydn's harmonic procedures here are so unusual that he dis-

penses with a key signature until the main theme returns in B major, halfway through the movement.

4. The through-composition of this quartet is explained in Webster, *Haydn's "Farewell" Symphony*, pp. 294–300, which quotes and amplifies Tovey's excellent discussion of the freedom of form in the Capriccio. Neither author, however, deals with the Capriccio as a conflation of two types of movement and the consequences of their interaction for the overall form.

5. Webster, *Haydn's "Farewell" Symphony*, p. 299. Webster's suggestion that the trio "distantly reminds us of the Capriccio" seems understated, but his notion of distance may also embrace the time gap: between the Capriccio and the Trio, the entire Menuet intervenes.

Chapter 7: Quartet in G Minor, Op. 20, No. 3

1. Keller, *The Great Haydn Quartets*, pp. 46–49; Landon, *Haydn: Chronicle and Works*, vol. 2, p. 332. Webster's parenthetic description of the whole quartet as "an eccentric composition even by Haydn's standards" serves, ironically, as preamble to an argument in favor of applying uniform bowing patterns to passages in the finale; see James Webster, "The Significance of Haydn's Quartet Autographs for Performance Practice," in *The String Quartets of Haydn, Mozart, and Beethoven* (Cambridge, MA: Harvard University Press, 1980), p. 77.

2. Though not specified in Haydn's autograph, a *forte* is implied at the beginning of the movement.

3. It is instructive to compare the Neapolitan sixth chord on the open C in bars 244–45 with the *fortissimo* diminished seventh, built on the cello's higher c, in bars 212–13. The Neapolitan passage is marked only *forte*, and that only in the cello part, but this is the second of two consecutive *forte* markings and probably means *più forte* in context. The strategic significance of the open C, as the last subdominant-orientated chord before the movement's definitive full close, thus could not be signaled more clearly.

4. Haydn uses a similar connection in his Quartet in C, op. 74, No. 1: the fifth of the V/vi chord at the end of the trio becomes the third of chord I in the reprise of the minuet. This late work (1793) differs from op. 17, No. 2, in that its trio, in the more remotely related key of A major, is a fully formed structure containing two harmonically balanced halves. Haydn writes an additional link passage to take the harmony from A major to the dominant of A minor, and thence back to the C major minuet.

5. Keller, *The Great Haydn Quartets*, p. 51.

6. Keller's attempt to solve the problem hinges on his contention that the G major coda of the minuet sounds less like a *tierce de Picardie* than a dominant chord that forecasts a new key; the end of the trio, by contrast, is saved by a "chordal metamorphosis," V/iv becoming i, which reverses the process at the end of the minuet, i becoming V/iv. The idea that the minuet ends on the dominant strikes me as wholly unconvincing, for the reasons I have given above, and on these grounds Keller's symmetry collapses.

7. Earlier editions of this quartet, including the Eulenburg miniature score, show repeat signs around the second half of the trio. There is no textual authority for the extra

repeat, but it may be a sign that editors felt uncomfortable about the passage. The same repeat signs in the more recent Doblinger miniature score, alleged to be based on Haydn's autograph manuscript, is an editorial mistake.

8. Tovey, "Haydn, Franz Joseph," p. 537.

Chapter 8: Quartet in D Major, Op. 20, No. 4

1. These distinctions are regrettably, but not surprisingly, ignored in the Eulenburg edition, which tends to regularize articulation and edit out other notational peculiarities.

2. For further discussion, see my article "Beethoven and the Open String", pp. 18–19.

3. The Op. 33 set is exceptional in the Haydn quartet canon for its inclusion of variation movements as finales (Nos. 5 and 6), a form more enthusiastically taken up by Mozart in his chamber music and piano concertos.

4. This is another detail that the Eulenburg score does not get right.

5. The Eulenberg score and older performing editions are especially faulty in the second half of the theme.

6. In other quartet movements, we sometimes encounter *cantabile* as a tempo or expression marking, and there is one instance of *innocentemente* and a movement entitled Fantasia. That does not, of course, mean that Haydn's quartets are generally devoid of exoticism, but rather that he rarely gives verbal clues to it. The slow movement of Op. 54, No. 2, is the most gypsy-like piece in all the quartets of Haydn, Mozart and Beethoven, but the composer, with characteristic understatement, marks it simply "Adagio."

7. Keller, *The Great Haydn Quartets*, pp. 55–56.

8. In *The* Style hongrois *in the Music of Western Europe* (Boston: Northeastern University Press, 1993), Jonathan Bellman ignores the intricate relationship between surface rhythms and meter when he suggests that "the appellation *Minuetto* [sic] *alla Zingarese* seems to mean nothing more than *pesante*" (p. 95).

9. Haydn was to repeat this artifice, though not in quite the same way, in the trio of his next quartet in D major, Op. 33, No. 6.

10. The dots in the cello part, in particular, suggest *spiccato*, the bow bouncing lightly on the string, with the recurring A taken on the open string. When Haydn transposes this passage up a fourth for the recapitulation, he sacrifices the possibility of open D strings (the *staccato* marks disappear, too), though the high register preserves the lightness of character.

Chapter 9: Quartet in E♭ Major, Op. 20, No. 1

1. Tovey, "Haydn, Franz Joseph," p. 534.

2. Tovey, "Haydn, Franz Joseph," p. 534; James Webster, "Mozart's and Haydn's Mutual Borrowings," in *Haydn Studies*, ed. Jens Peter Larsen, Howard Serwer, and James Webster (New York: Norton, 1980), p. 411; Keller, *The Great Haydn Quartets*, pp. 30–31. Keller also claims to have "circumstantial evidence" that Brahms knew Op. 20, No. 1 intimately, but does not provide it; it may be that he had the Beethoven copy in mind but attributed it incorrectly.

3. Not even a subtlety of this order seems to have escaped the eyes of editors bent on standardizing Haydn's articulation: in the Eulenburg score, the viola and cello slurs in bar 4 uniformly cover the four eighth notes!

4. Webster, *Haydn's "Farewell" Symphony*, p. 161.

5. In other words, phrases that are multiples of four bars are perceived as regular because the ear is reluctant to "hear against" the equilibrium of a natural order. Phrases built from an odd number of bars sound irregular because it is difficult for the listener to settle on a single metrical reading. My phrase analysis of the exposition and development is thus only one of a number of possibilities: it is difficult to say whether bars 19 and 24 belong to the four bars separating them, or whether one—or both—should be grouped to the music preceding and following them, respectively. This is not to say that the "development section" is free of metrical ambiguity—the music on either side of bar 60 is problematical—but rather that it is *possible* for the ear to comprehend much of it as flowing along in regular four-bar groups.

6. Webster, "The Bass Part in Haydn's Early String Quartets," pp. 403, 417–19.

7. The move towards the cadence at the end of Example 9.12 gives a further instance of part-crossing, that of the viola below the cello: the only way to make sense of the bass line is to regard the viola as an octave too high. The crossing arises not from the danger of consecutives but because Haydn apparently wants a strong sonority for the entry of the lower strings after two bars' rest. The cello cannot supply a low G if it wishes to link up with the accompaniment before the violin solo, which was broken off on a♭.

8. The repeat of the second half is authentic; the Eulenburg score mistakenly omits it.

9. In the Eulenburg edition of the miniature score as well as in older editions of the parts, the repeated notes straddling the bar line in the *(b)* form have been slurred together, obliterating the distinction between the *(a)* and *(b)* forms of syncopation.

10. The function of the slur is analogous to Haydn's instruction in the cello part of Op. 77, No. 2 (first movement, bars 92–93)—*l'istesso tuono* (the same tone)—though the cellist is additionally asked to change fingers. For more on this passage, see my article "Fingering in Haydn's String Quartets," p. 50.

11. In Example 9.18b, the violins' upbeat merely leads back to the middle of the movement for the repeat of the development and recapitulation; the fermata over their eighth rests marks the end of the piece following this repeat. Earlier editors either misunderstood this sign or could not believe that Haydn's appoggiatura-chord—supported by an apocryphal decrescendo to *pianissimo*—was meant to be played twice.

Chapter 10: Epilogue

1. See, for instance, Tovey, *Essays and Lectures on Music*, p. 275.

2. By comparison, the four Op. 50 finales in 2/4 meter are each over 200 bars long, and the other 6/8 finale contains 132 bars. One should not be misled by the tempo marking of the Op. 50, No. 4, in the Eulenburg score, which erroneously reads "Allegro moderato" instead of "Allegro molto."

3. The idea that the this fugue is capricious in character has a false ring, despite the joint claims of Webster, Finscher and Kirkendale (see Webster, *Haydn's "Farewell"*

Symphony, p. 295). As shown in chapter 3, the counterpoint is certainly as tight here as in the other quartets, and the overall design offers no surprises. It may be that these writers have in mind the sound of resonating open strings, which, as I showed earlier, are exploited in the more obviously *scherzando* opening movement; this is a consequence of Haydn's writing a piece whose first and final movements are in the same key.

4. That the opus of six works, not the single quartet, is ultimately the artistic unit here underlies much of László Somfai's discussion of the ordering of works in an opus in the "Excursus" to his study "An Introduction to the Study of Haydn's String Quartet Autographs," published in *The String Quartets of Haydn, Mozart, and Beethoven: Studies of the Autograph Manuscripts*, ed. Christoph Wolff (Cambridge, MA: Harvard University Press, 1980); see especially pp. 11–16.

5. Somfai, "An Introduction to the Study of Haydn's String Quartet Autographs," p. 36.

6. The dedication of Op. 50 (1787) to a royal cellist, King Friedrich Wilhelm II of Prussia, does not seem to have had much influence on Haydn's distribution of thematic materials among the four parts, certainly nothing like the effect it was to have on Mozart's three "Prussian" quartets of a few years later. Admittedly, there is a variation-movement theme (in Op. 50, No. 3) in which the cello is accompanied from below by the viola for eight bars. This is hardly a striking use of the instrument in comparison with the opening movement and Capriccio of Op. 20, No. 2, or the soaring arpeggios in the finale of Op. 54, No. 2, in C, which was composed for a violin virtuoso a year after the six dedicated to the king.

Bibliography

Editions of Haydn's String Quartets

83 String Quartets by Josef Haydn. 3 vols. Ed. Wilhelm Altmann. London: Eulenburg, n.d. [miniature scores].

Haydn: Quartette. 4 vols. New York, London, and Frankfurt: C. F. Peters. Vols. 1–2 as *30 berühmte Quartette . . . von Joseph Haydn.* Ed. Andreas Moser and Hugo Deschert, ca. 1918. Vols. 3–4, n.d. [parts].

Joseph Haydn: Streichquartette. Ed. Reginald Barrett-Ayres and H. C. Robbins Landon. Vienna: Doblinger, ca. 1977–87 [miniature scores].

Joseph Haydn: Werke. Ed. Joseph-Haydn Institut, Cologne, series xii. Munich: Henle, 1963– [scores and critical commentary].

Literature and other editions of music

Baillot, Pierre. *L'art du violon.* Paris: Imprimerie du Conservatoire de Musique, 1834.

Bellman, Jonathan. *The* Style hongrois *in the Music of Western Europe.* Boston: Northeastern University Press, 1993.

Brandenburg, Sieghard, ed. *Ludwig van Beethoven: Briefwechsel Gesamtausgabe.* 7 vols. Munich: Henle, 1996–98.

Drabkin, William. "Beethoven and the Open String." *Music Analysis* 4 (1985), pp. 15–28.

———. "Beethoven's Understanding of 'Sonata Form': The Evidence of the Sketchbooks." In *Beethoven's Compositional Process*, ed. W. Kinderman, pp. 14–19. Lincoln: University of Nebraska Press, 1991.

———. "The Cello Part in Beethoven's Late Quartets." *Beethoven Forum* 7 (1999), pp. 45–66.

————. "Fingering in Haydn's Quartets." *Early Music* 16 (1988), pp. 50–57.

Feder, Georg. Worklist for "Haydn, (Franz) Joseph." In *The New Grove Dictionary of Music and Musicians*, ed. Stanley Sadie, vol. 8, pp. 378–79. London: Macmillan, 1980.

Finscher, Ludwig. *Studien zur Geschichte des Streichquartetts, I: Die Enstehung des klassichen Streichquartetts, von den Vorformen zur Grundlegung durch Joseph Haydn*. Kassel: Bärenreiter, 1974.

Gotwals, Vernon, ed. and trans. *Haydn: Two Contemporary Portraits*. Madison: University of Wisconsin Press, 1968.

Jacob, Heinrich Eduard. *Joseph Haydn: Seine Kunst, seine Zeit, sein Ruhm*. Hamburg: Wegener, 1954.

Keller, Hans. *The Great Haydn Quartets: Their Interpretation*. London: Dent, 1986.

Kirkendale, Warren. *Fugue and Fugato in Rococo and Classical Chamber Music*. Durham, NC: Duke University Press, 1979.

Landon, H. C. Robbins. *Haydn: Chronicle and Works*. 5 vols. London: Thames and Hudson, 1976–80.

Larsen, Jens Peter, Howard Serwer and James Webster, eds. *Haydn Studies*. New York: Norton, 1980.

Lenz, Wilhelm von. *Beethoven, eine Kunststudie*. 5 vols. Hamburg: Hoffmann and Campe, 1855–60.

Levy, Janet. "Texture as a Sign in Classic and Early Romantic Music." *Journal of the American Musicological Society* 35 (1982), pp. 482–531.

Mozart, Leopold. *Gründliche Violinschule*. 1756. 3rd edition. Augsburg: Lotte, 1787. Facsimile reprint, ed. H. J. Moser, Leipzig: Brietkopf und Härtel, 1956. English trans. by Editha Knocker as *Treatise on Violin Playing*, 2nd edition. London: Oxford University Press, 1951.

Ordonez, Carlo d'. *String Quartets, Opus 1*. Ed. A. Peter Brown. Madison: AR Editions, 1980.

Quantz, Johann Joachim. *Versuch einer Anweisung, die Flöte traversiere zu spielen*. Berlin: Voss, 1752. English trans by Edward R. Reilley as *On Playing the Flute*, London: Faber and Faber, 1966.

Richter, Frantisek Xaver. *Divertimenti per quartetto d'archi*. Musica Antiqua Bohemica 71. Prague: Editio Supraphon, 1969.

Rosen, Charles. *The Classical Style*. London: Faber and Faber, 1971.

————. *Sonata Forms*, 2nd edition. New York: Norton, 1988.

Somfai, László, "An Introduction to the Study of Haydn's String Quartet Autographs." In *The String Quartets of Haydn, Mozart, and Beethoven: Studies of the Autograph Manuscripts*, ed. Christoph Wolff, pp. 5–51. Cambridge, MA: Harvard University Press, 1980.

Stowell, Robin. *Violin Technique and Performance Practice in the Late Eighteenth and Early Nineteenth Centuries*. Cambridge: Cambridge University Press, 1983.

Sutcliffe, W. Dean. *Haydn: String Quartets, Op. 50*. Cambridge: Cambridge University Press, 1992.

Tovey, Donald F. *Beethoven*. Ed. Hubert J. Foss. London: Oxford University Press, 1944.

————. *Essays and Lectures on Music.* Ed. Hubert Foss. London: Oxford University Press, 1949.

————. "Haydn, Franz Joseph." In *Cobbett's Cyclopedic Survey of Chamber Music*, ed. W. W. Cobbett. London: Oxford University Press, 1929. Reprinted in *Essays and Lectures on Music.*

————. *Musical Articles from the Encyclopaedia Britannica.* London: Oxford University Press, 1944.

Webster, James. "The Bass Part in Haydn's Early String Quartets." *Musical Quarterly* 63 (1977), pp. 390–424.

————. "The Chronology of Haydn's String Quartets." *Musical Quarterly* 61 (1975), pp. 17–46.

————. "Freedom of Form in Haydn's Early String Quartets." In *Haydn Studies*, ed. Jens Peter Larsen, Howard Serwer, and James Webster, pp. 522–30. New York: Norton, 1980.

————. *Haydn's "Farewell" Symphony and the Idea of Classical Style.* Cambridge: Cambridge University Press, 1991.

————. "Mozart's and Haydn's Mutual Borrowings." In *Haydn Studies,* ed. Jens Peter Larsen, Howard Serwer, and James Webster, pp. 410–12. New York: Norton, 1980.

————. "The Significance of Haydn's Quartet Autographs for Performance Practice," in *The String Quartets of Haydn, Mozart, and Beethoven: Studies of the Autograph Manuscripts*, ed. Christoph Wolff, pp. 62–95. Cambridge, MA: Harvard University Press, 1980.

————. "Towards a History of Viennese Chamber Music in the Early Classical Period." *Journal of the American Musicological Society* 27 (1974), pp. 212–47.

————. "Violoncello and Double Bass in the Chamber Music of Haydn and His Viennese Contemporaries, 1750–1780." *Journal of the American Musicological Society* 29 (1976), pp. 413–38.

Index

acciaccature as part of gypsy style, 139
Albrechtsberger, Johann Georg, 68
alla Zingarese (gypsy style), 125, 137–
    39, 141–42, 176 n. 6, 176 n. 8
alla zoppa, 137
al rovescio (inversion), 52, 54, 57–58,
    61, 63
antecedent and consequent phrase
    construction, 17, 48, 54, 69, 133,
    149, 156
antiphonal textures, 17–20, 39, 50, 107,
    110, 113, 128, 130, 140–41, 144,
    146, 148
aria, 21–24, 29, 39, 81, 86–88, 169 nn. 7–8

Bach, Carl Philipp Emanuel, sonata with
    varied reprises, 40, 86–87
Bach, Johann Sebastian Bach, *Well-
    Tempered Clavier*, 55
Baillot, Pierre, 170 n. 14
bariolage, 44–45, 120–21
Beethoven, Ludwig van: early chamber
    music, 46, 143; influence of Mozart
    and Haydn, 9; late quartets, 3
    WORKS:
    piano sonatas: Op. 2, No. 2 (A), 84;
        Op. 7 (E♭), 46; Op. 14, No. 1 (E),

arranged for quartet, 10, 168 n. 1,
    170 n. 18; Op. 106 "Hammer-
    klavier" (B♭), 67, 162; Op. 111 (c),
    46–47
string quartets: Op. 18, No. 5 (A), 84;
    Op. 59, No. 3 (C), 51, Op. 130/133
    with "Grosse Fuge" (B♭), 67, 162;
    Op. 131 (c♯), 162
symphonies: No. 5 (c), 162; No. 9 (d),
    162
Bellman, Jonathan, 176 n. 8
Blume, Friedrich, 171 n. 1
Brahms, Johannes, 161, 176 n. 2(b)
Brown, A. Peter, 172 n. 13

cadenza, 73, 87, 120, 136–37, 144
canon, 54–56, 58, 66, 171 n. 8
cello as melodic instrument, 33–35, 38,
    91–92, 94, 101, 118–20, 125, 135–
    36, 139, 145, 170 n. 12, 178 n. 6
Choa, Sharon, 172 n. 9
chorale texture, 35
chromatic harmony, 30–33, 55, 71–73,
    95
concerto grosso, 66
con forza, 115
con sordino (with mute), 14, 45, 171 n. 19

deceptive cadence, 26, 31, 137
double stopping, 39–41, 103

episode, fugal, 52–54, 65
exposition, fugal, 52–54, 63–64, 144,
    172 n. 9

false reprise, 125, 128, 130, 132, 150,
    153
fantasia, 97–99, 174 n. 3b
Feder, Georg, ix
figured bass, 78
finale as culmination, 161–62, 177 n. 2
Finscher, Ludwig, viii, 167 n. 1, 171 n. 1,
    177 n. 3(b)
Friedrich Wilhelm II, King of Prussia,
    178 n. 6
fugue, 30, 51–68, 91–94, 144–5
Fux, Johann-Joseph, 60

galant style, 24, 51–52, 54, 64, 67, 95,
    133, 162
gavotte, 138
Goethe, Johann Wolfgang von, 3, 17, 168
    n. 6
gypsy style (alla Zingarese), 125, 137–
    39, 141–42, 176 n. 6, 176 n. 8

Handel, Messiah, chorus "And with His
    Stripes," 55, 172 n. 8
Haydn, Franz Joseph: "celebrated"
    quartets, 91; "early" quartet,
    definition of, viii–ix; faulty editions
    of quartets, 168 n. 3, 174 n. 1(b),
    175 n. 7, 176 nn. 1(a), 4, 5, 177 nn.
    3(b)a, 8, 9, 11, 2; keyboard style in
    quartets, 11; and "Op. 3," 171 n.
    19; Op. 33 as "composed in a new
    and special way," 164–65, 169 n. 7;
    ordering of quartets in an opus, 52,
    163–64, 171 n. 21; quartet canon
    and chronology, 1–2; sketches and
    drafts, 119–120
    WORKS:

string quartets: Op. 1, No. 1 (B♭), 4–7,
    12, 18–19, 21–22, 29, 41; Op. 1,
    No. 2 (E♭), 42; Op. 1, No. 3 (D),
    12–14, 18, 41; Op. 1, No. 4 (G),
    14–16, 18, 45; Op. 1, No. 6 (C), 45,
    171 n. 19; Op. 2, No. 1 (A), 19, 41;
    Op. 2, No. 2 (E), 39, 44–45; Op. 2,
    No. 4 (F), 35, 170 n. 18; Op. 9, No.
    1 (C), 11, 24–26, 43, 77, 115; Op. 9,
    No. 2 (E♭), 22–23, 68, 164, 174 n.
    4; Op. 9, No. 3 (G), 30, 43, 156;
    Op. 9, No. 4 (d), 31, 40, 70–71, 81,
    164, 174 n. 4; Op. 9, No. 5 (B♭),
    35–38, 68, 118, 133, 152; Op. 9,
    No. 6 (A), 26–27, 43–44, 81, 85;
    Op. 17, No. 1 (E), 28–29, 68, 156;
    Op. 17, No. 2 (F), 31–32, 38–39,
    68, 115–16, 156, 175 n. 4(b); Op.
    17, No. 3 (E♭), 35, 152–53; Op. 17,
    No. 4 (c), 35, 40, 117, 152, 164,
    174 n. 4; Op. 17, No. 5 (G), 22–23,
    27–28, 68, 156, 164; Op. 17, No. 6
    (D), 68, 81, 156; Op. 20, No. 1,
    115–16, 143–59, 164; Op. 20, No. 2
    (C), 30, 38, 50, 52–54, 63–68, 91–
    104, 125, 148, 162–63, 178 n. 6;
    Op. 20, No. 3 (g), 38, 105–24; Op.
    20, No. 4 (D), 30, 33–34, 125–42,
    164; Op. 20, No. 5 (f), 30–31, 47–
    48, 52–59, 61, 66, 69–80, 162, 173
    n. 4; Op. 20, No.6 (A), 38, 52–54,
    59–63, 66, 81–90, 162–63, 172 n.
    12, 174 n. 4; Op. 33, No. 1 (b), 38;
    Op. 33, No. 2 (E♭), 38, 47, 170 n.
    12; Op. 33, No. 3 (C), 90, 174 n. 4;
    Op. 33, No. 4 (B♭), 170 n. 16; Op.
    33, No. 5 (G), 10, 24, 79, 173 n. 4;
    Op. 33, No. 6 (D), 33–34, 176 n. 9;
    Op. 50, No. 1 (B♭), 79; Op. 50, No.
    3 (E♭), 33, 170 n. 2, 178 n. 6; Op.
    50, No. 4 (f♯), 53, 58–59, 162, 172
    n. 9; Op. 50, No. 5 (F), 152; Op. 50,
    No. 6 (D), 44; Op. 54, No. 2 (C),
    173 n. 3, 178 n. 6; Op. 54, No. 3

(E), 118, 171 n. 20; Op. 55, No. 1
(A), 2; Op. 55, No. 2 (f), 133; Op.
64, No. 1 (C), 34–35; Op. 64, No. 4
(G), 44; Op. 64, No. 5 (D), 52, 118;
Op. 64, No. 6 (E♭), 38, 52; Op. 71,
No. 1 (B♭), 49–50, 79; Op. 71, No.
3 (E♭), 52; Op. 74, No. 1 (C), 175 n.
4(b); Op. 76, No. 2 (d), 48–49, 80;
Op. 76, No. 6 (E♭), 133, 174 n. 3(b);
Op. 77, No. 2 (F), 177 n. 10
symphonies: No. 7 "Le midi" (C), 22
trios for violin, viola, baryton: No. 97
(D), 171 n. 2, No. 101 (C), 171 n. 2,
No. 107 (D), 168 n. 4, No. 114 (D),
171 n. 2
Holz, Karl, 3, 168 n. 7

"ideal" textures and themes, 45–50, 73,
95, 126
incomplete structures, 115–18, 150–51,
175 n. 4(b)
interpolation, phrase, 108–9
inversion (al rovescio) 52, 54, 57–58, 61,
63

Keller, Hans, 2–3, 117, 138, 171 n. 19,
173 n. 4, 175 n. 6, 176 n. 2(b)
Kirkendale, Warren, 171 nn. 2–3, 172 n.
13, 177 n. 3b

Landon, H. C. Robbins, 2, 167 n. 1, 171
n. 21
Levy, Janet, 169 n. 10
l'istesso tuono, 177 n. 10
Liszt, Franz, 161

Mendelssohn, Felix: influence of Mozart
and Beethoven, 9
messa di voce, 26–29, 74, 92
movements, interrelationships between,
101–102, 153, 156, 161–63, 175 n.
5(a)
Mozart, Leopold, 169 n. 9, 170 n. 17
Mozart, Wolfgang Amadè: cello melo-

dies in "Prussian" quartets, 33, 178
n. 6; quartets modeled on Haydn, 9
WORKS:
oboe quartet K. 370 (F), 173 n. 3
piano quartets: K. 478 (g), 17–18
string quartets: K. 387 (G), 17–19, 51,
171 n. 6, 172 n. 13; K. 421 (d), 79;
K. 428 (E♭), 143
string quintets: K. 516 (g), 171 n. 19
symphonies: K. 551 "Jupiter" (C), 162
mute (con sordino), 14, 45, 171 n. 19

open strings, 43–44, 75–76, 81, 94, 103,
110, 118, 132, 152, 155, 170 nn. 12,
18, 176 n. 10, 177–78, n. 3
Ordonez, Carlo d', 171 n. 2, 172 n. 13

parallel motion, 49–50, 61, 64, 95, 122,
128, 131, 134–36, 149, 155–156
pedal points, 103–4
perdendosi, 113
per figuram retardationis, 78–79
performance, 118, 132, 139, 169 n. 6,
176 n. 10
pizzicato, 40–42, 80
portamento, 38
portato, 46, 80, 98, 127, 129

Quantz, Johann Joachim, 169 n. 9
quartet-divertimento, 167 n. 1

recitative, 22–23, 169 n. 6
"redundant" entry, fugal, 54, 61, 64
register as compositional resource, 25,
34–38, 41, 63, 74, 81–82, 90, 95,
103, 106, 129–30, 134, 146, 149,
154, 156, 176 n. 10
retardatio, 78
Richter, Frantisek Xaver, 68, 171 n. 2,
172 n. 13
ritornello, 66, 99, 101
Rosen, Charles, 168 n. 5(a), 171 n. 20

Sandberger, Adolf, 171 n. 1

Schumann, Robert, 161
serenade, 40–42, 76
siciliano, 24–26, 77, 79, 169 n. 8, 173 n. 4
Somfai, László, 163, 178 n. 4
sonata form, and fugue, 51–52, 58, 110–11
Stowell, Robin, 170 n. 14
stretto in fugue, 52, 54–56, 58, 60, 62, 66, 95
Sturm und Drang, 143
Sutcliffe, W. Dean, 59, 167 n. 1, 169 n. 6
symphony, 12, 29, 39
syncopation, 156

tempo markings, 151–52, 173 n. 4, 176 n. 6
tierce de Picardie, 114, 175 n. 6
Tovey, Donald F., 21, 52, 84, 118, 133, 161, 174 n. 2(b)

trio sonata, 4, 12–16, 39, 50, 73, 76, 91–92, 112–13, 136, 144, 146, 148

una corda, sopra, 38–39, 82–83, 90, 103
ungaresca, 137
unison textures, 29–30, 37, 42, 46, 63, 102, 106, 122, 126, 132, 137, 144

variation movements, 133–37, 176 n. 3
vibrato, 132

Waldstein, Count Ferdinand von, 9
Webster, James, 167 nn. 1, 5, 169 n. 11, 170 n. 13, 171 n. 1, 172 n. 11; 175, nn. 4(a), 5(a), 177 n. 3b
Werner, Gregor, 172 n. 13

Zelter, Carl Friedrich, 168

About the Author

WILLIAM DRABKIN is Senior Lecturer in Music at the University of Southampton in England. He has written books on Beethoven and Schenkerian analysis and serves on the editorial board of two journals, *Music Analysis* and *Beethoven Forum*.

ISBN 0-313-30173-5

90000>

9 780313 301735

EAN

HARDCOVER BAR CODE